CHESTER BYERS.

Cowboy Roping and Rope Tricks

BY

CHESTER BYERS

WITH CONTRIBUTIONS BY
FRED STONE, WILL ROGERS AND ELSIE JANIS

Illustrated

DOVER PUBLICATIONS, INC.
NEW YORK

This Dover edition, first published in 1966, is an unabridged republication of the work first published by G. P. Putnam's Sons in 1928. This work has been previously published under the title *Roping: Trick and Fancy Rope Spinning.*

International Standard Book Number: 0-486-25711-8

Dover Publications, Inc.
31 East 2nd Street
Mineola, New York 11501

FOREWORD

by
WILL ROGERS

CHET sent me word he was going to write a book. Well he wasn't where I could get at him to choke him off, and then agin he is of what they call "lawful age, free born and sound of mind and body," that is he is as sound of mind as a man can be who spends the best part of his life making rings with a piece of rope and going through life trying to jump through em, then when he does get through on the other side he immediately wants to get back on the side he just come from.

Now I can't give a man much "marking" on his intellect, when he will continually keep doing a thing like that. But it's just men and women that do fool things like that, that write all these books. So just let Chet take his old trick rope and start whipping it down on some good white paper, I

don't know how tangled up he is liable to get in it,
I do know this, that statistics have never shown
where any trick roper, for the good of posterity
has ever been fortunate enough to choke himself
with his own rope.

I doubt if the book will be any good, for it's on
a subject. And all the books I ever read on sub-
jects were written by men that dident know anything about the subject. And people read them
and think they are pretty good. So I hate to
see Chet pick out the subject of Ropes. I would
have had more confidence in it if he had picked
out something that he dident know anything
about.

Now Chet knows ropes, and Chet knows Roping,
so it is liable to be awful uninteresting, and be con-
tradicted by the 109 million that dont know roping.
So Chet shows he dont know nothing about
Authoring right there.

When I write my books I always pick out something I know absolutely nothing about, then when
the people read it, they think it is right, for there
is more people in this Country that are wrong,
than there are that are right. So keep em wrong,
if they was right they wouldent know it. So

FOREWORD

Chet's old book is liable to be "hay-wire" right from the first loop he spills.

I hope roping is easier to read about than it is to do. I tried it one time and the rope all twists up on me. I hope he tells

What to do when it gets all tangled up in your hands.

Do you let it twist in your hand or hold it tight?

What kind of rope do you use for catching and not for missing?

Is some animals like women, easier caught than others?

Why is it that Trick Ropers carry their own horses? Is it because they have them trained to run into the loop? I have never seen one trick roping at a Bronk.

Do you think the rider has anything to do with a trick roper's success, or is it just luck?

Has anybody that has ever become afflicted with trick roping ever been cured of it? When? How? and Where?

Which end of a rope is the best to make a loop in?

How far can you throw a rope and miss anything?

FOREWORD

How close to the Judges do you have to be to win a trick roping Contest?

Do trick Ropers ever miss purposely, or is all that missing accidental?

What color horse is better for the tail catch?

Will a half inch rope make as big a loop as a three quarter inch one will?

When you make a loop and dont want to jump in it, or through it, what do you do with it?

Why do some ropers use larger loops than others, is it because they are more ambitious and want to catch more?

Suppose you throw a rope right at a calf's head, and he moves it after you throw, and it aint there when your rope gets there, who's fault is that, yours, or the calf's?

If you don't throw directly at his head and he sees it coming and dodges into it, is that an error on his part, or is that mind reading on yours?

How long do you have to do a trick before you get it so you never miss it in your life?

How long will a man keep missing before he will turn to honest work?

Now you needent answer these Chet till the next Volume, you will have to write another volume to explain what you meant in this one, all Authors do that.

Chet told me that he wanted to show where rope spinning was healthful and benefitial. Well maby it is, I dont know, I have tried it a good deal, and there was lots of days I dident feel good, and after I would go out and miss awhile I wouldent feel any better.

Course every man to his own feelings, What might make you feel good would make me feel rotten, chances are it would. So I dont know nothing about your health, maby roping would do it good, maby quinine or pills would do it good, Lord I got enough trouble worrying about my own health, to be messing around bothering about what would be good for yours.

If Byers wants to tell the world whats the matter with them, why he's got as much right to do it as anybody, I would trust his judgment just as quick as I would a Chiropodist. Maby the World needs Rope spinning, I dont know, I know it needs something, nothing they can learn and do will be any worse for it than the stuff it is doing now, It may keep you out of some other kind of devilment. Just as well be doing rope spinning as the black bottom. Maby rope spinning is our Country's future salvation, I know it hasent any the speed its moving at now. It takes both hands to rope so you certainly cant be drinking and do it, so that is one big advantage to modern civilization right now there. It dont cost much, only court plaster and colodium (or new skin).

If you dont get roping perfect, why dont be discouraged, for nobody else has. Its better than Golf for it aint going to make a liar out of you. You can learn it in the house, its heartily endorsed by the light fixture, and furniture people.

Now I dont know what Chet has told you in this book, thats why I am a friend to so many Authors I never read their books. But whatever he has told you, is so.

Chet knows more about roping than any man in the world. He is one man in his line that is absolute Champion. He is what I would call a "natural" roper, what I mean by that he does everything "right" with a rope, he dont do anything "wrong."

I dont mean he dont miss, Lord they all miss even me, Course I havent missed a roping trick for years, but the old timers will set around and tell you back in the old days when I went for a trick and missed it, course I recovered and did it the next trial but I DID MISS.

I only have two things that I will always die very proud of, one of them was that I used to teach Chet Byers tricks with a rope, and the other was that I waved at the train that Queen Marie was on, and I will always believe she saw me.

Now I dont want you to think that I am in anyway kinder cold feet, on this plan of Chets where it will help you, and build you up, it may do it. When I first knew Chet and he was just starting it, he wouldent weigh over eighty pounds, a poor skinny little man of fourteen years of age.

This roping has built him up and added twenty-five years and over a hundred pounds in weight to him. Course the food he ate might have had something to do with it, But I doubt it. I lay the best part of his tonnage, and age to Rope spinning.

Course on the other hand it hasent done anything for me, I am as young as I ever was, and am getting lighter every day so its hard to tell.

FOREWORD

So get a rope and start missing, Thats about 80 per cent of all there is to roping. Its great exercise if you want to get tired, personally I dont care to get tired, If I am rested I would rather stay that way.

WILL ROGERS.

WILL ROGERS.

FRED STONE DOES HIS STUFF.

READY.   "WEDDING RING."

"UP AND OVER."   NOTHING TO IT!

WARNING!

WELL, here are a few pictures of me spinning a rope when Chester Byers was teaching me. But it don't show me tangling the rope around my neck or biting it and throwing it down and stamping it as I would a snake. I did all of that, too; for it got my goat many times. Spinning a rope certainly is real exercise.

Now listen, audience, if you ever start roping and learn the first trick (The Wedding Ring), *you're gone*. You will never rest till you know more about ropes, loops, hondas, rope-spinning, straight roping and which cowboy is the best. In fact you'll tear for a ranch to learn more and get in the atmosphere of the real out-door life. I'm telling you.

ELSIE JANIS.

ADVICE

by

Elsie Janis

I am extremely proud and happy to be among those present in Mr. Byers' little book on ropology. For years I've been suffering from chronic "lariatitis" and I don't seem to get any better, or any worse. But I certainly enjoy it. And I marvel at the fact that more people haven't caught it.

It's great exercise, and personally I would rather twirl a rope than jump one. Of course, experts like Messrs. Byers, Rogers, and Stone, can do both at the same time, but it takes a lot of practice.

It is odd that more women don't go in for roping, because it is really not as hard as going around a golf course in ninety as some of my girl friends do. But even in the west on ranches I found very few girls who could handle a rope well. Some say

ADVICE

they are afraid of developing too strong a muscle in the right arm. But I've been roping for twelve years and have nothing to show that would cause Mr. Tunney any pangs of envy.

I find it exhilarating and its possibilities are unlimited, for no matter how many tricks you think you know along comes Mr. Byers, and you realize you don't know "nuthin." Years ago he tried to show me how to make a butterfly with the rope. I'm still trying, but I can't seem to get beyond the cocoon stage. However, when this little book comes out I shall start all over again because I'm sure if any one can explain the catches in the lariat business Mr. Byers can.

I hope to see the ladies step up and take notice. And to any one starting in, I offer a few don'ts— leaving the "dos" to Mr. Byers.

Don't start in the drawing room, unless it's some one else's house.

Don't wear a dress for which you have any future plans.

Don't get discouraged if you nearly hang yourself—be glad you didn't succeed in doing so.

Don't expect to do Will Rogers' act the first

ADVICE

week. It took me two months and I'm fairly quick at grabbing other people's stuff.

Good luck, Mr. Byers, and long may your lariat wave.

CONTENTS

CONTENTS

ILLUSTRATIONS

ROPING

ROPING

CHAPTER I

PRINCIPLES OF ROPE SPINNING

SPINNING a rope is the science or sport of throwing a short rope in such a way that a portion of it is dilated into a loop. This loop rotates in front of the roper or is swung about the body in various stunts and tricks.

For a beginner the ordinary trick lariat or spinning rope is about 14 feet long. At one end it is whipped or stopped to prevent unravelling. At the other end there is an eye, commonly called the "honda" through which the rope is run, thus making a loop. It is this loop in various forms that is used in the far West to lasso cattle. In the present text this loop is used as part of the sport of spinning.

The principle of rope spinning is that the centri-

3

fugal force of the loop distends it in such a way that it will lie open in midair as long as revolved. To begin a loop the rope must, therefore, be cast from the hands of the roper in such a way that it starts whirling at once and before it touches the ground. The friction of the spoke, or free end, against the *honda* prevents the loop from closing.

It will be seen in the various tricks that the diameter of the loop varies. For most tricks a small loop is desirable revolving at low speed.

For tricks in which the loop is to be revolved about the body or to be jumped through while revolving in a vertical plane the loop should be large.

In developing these various tricks and stunts with the loop famous cowboys have used various styles and weights of ropes. In learning the sport of rope spinning it is desirable to keep as nearly as possible to a small form of *honda* and a rope of medium weight.

The average convenient size of a spinning rope for a beginner is ⅜ of an inch in diameter; length, 14 feet. As the spinner improves he should go to a 20 or 25 foot rope to permit bigger loops.

The rope should *not* be what is known as a "laid

ROPE TYPES.

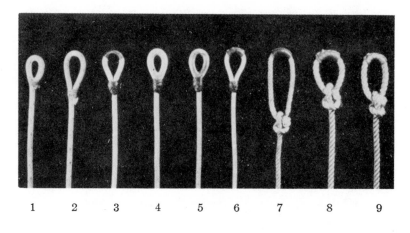

| 1 | 2 | 3 | 4 | 5 | 6 | 7 | 8 | 9 |

SOME FORMS OF SPINNING ROPES AND LASSOS.

Nos. 1, 2 and 3 are ropes usually used by the amateur. They are braided and usually size 12 rope, or ⅜ inch in diameter.

No. 1 has a honda of brass or aluminum cut thin for lightness. No. 2 has no metal honda. No. 3 has the honda weighted by the addition of a few turns of copper wire.

* * * *

Nos. 4, 5 and 6 are also braided rope. No. 4 is a thicker rope having a heavy aluminum honda. This adds weight enough to enable the spinner to dilate a very large loop, say 10 to 15 ft. in diameter. No. 6 has no metal honda, but is reinforced with leather so that the loop in the eye will not wear.

* * * *

Nos. 7, 8 and 9 are the rough heavy made ropes which are used in cattle work by mounted cowboys. The honda is simply an eye formed by tying a knot, which is reinforced with rawhide or leather.

* * * *

There are ropes and hondas almost without number. But for the amateur spinner a braided rope is best because it does not kink so readily; and a light honda of brass or aluminum gives the small loop and proper balance. Nos. 1, 2 and 3 are therefore best adapted to the beginner.

rope" such as the ordinary hemp rope which has strands in a spiral. The loop rope is a braided rope commonly called a sash cord. This method of manufacture makes a loop more pliable and less likely to kink.

CHAPTER II

(*Rope Spinning in a Horizontal Plane*)

Introduction:

Flat loops are so called because the loop revolves in a horizontal plane. This form of spinning is the simplest. A large or small loop can also be used. And it can be revolved forward (clockwise) or backward (counter-clockwise), that is to say to the left or right.

It is suggested that the beginner try the loop first left and then right, that is, forward and then backward. This helps because as the loop revolves the rope will tend to wind up and kink. Kinking is best overcome by letting the spoke, or free end, twist in the hand and thus reduce or altogether avoid the winding up and kinking.

1. Flat loop—forward (left spin).

Stand with the feet placed slightly apart, body bent forward at the waist, arms down below waist

6

FIGURE 1—(a). FLAT LOOP—FORWARD (LEFT SPIN).

Stand with the feet placed slightly apart. Body bent slightly forward at the waist. Arms down below waist and held comfortably but slightly before the body as shown in diagram. (See Page 9).

and held comfortably but slightly before the body as shown in Fig. 1.

As the diagram indicates, the loop held in the two hands can be of a convenient diameter depending on the height of the spinner. The spoke (the part of the rope between the right hand and the *honda*) should be about equal to the radius of the loop. Thus for a three foot loop the right hand should be about 18 inches from the *honda*. The left hand holds both the loop and the continuation of the spoke. The fingers of the left hand should be loose so that the rope can be dropped quickly as the whirling starts.

Now throw the right hand in a counter-clockwise direction slightly away from the body, at the same time releasing the loop with both hands and holding the guiding spoke with the fingers of the right hand. Meanwhile the left hand has held on just long enough to let the loop get started clear of the body and the whirl begin. The spoke hand (right) should be held far enough from the body so that the loop does not strike the legs or clothing.

The right hand, now holding the spoke, describes a circular movement, revolving counter-

9

clockwise. This causes the loop to continue open by centrifugal force and to whirl about with the spoke acting roughly both as its radius and its support.

At this point the beginner must stop and practice for some minutes or longer until he has mastered the small loop. The problem is not so much one of speed, as one of *rhythm*. Just as the timing of a baseball bat or a golf club is the secret of a home run or a long drive, so it is the rhythm of the spoke hand in spinning which is the secret of the skillful rope spinner.

The beginner also must remember at this point that the spinning of the loop, gripped too tightly, causes the rope to twist and so to kink. To overcome this he will find it a simple matter to let the spoke turn in his hand so that almost no kinking results. Sometimes the left hand, which may still hold the continuation of the spoke, can assist in this turning. Then try the next spin backward or to the right. This will untwist the rope.

In all exercises with the rope an excellent practice is to learn to do the various tricks as slowly as possible.

FIGURE I—(b). FLAT LOOP—FORWARD (LEFT SPIN).

The right hand, now holding the spoke, describes a circular movement, revolving counter-clockwise. This causes the loop to continue open by centrifugal force and to whirl about with the spoke acting roughly both as its radius and its support. (See Page 9).

2. Flat loop—backward (right spin).

The flat loop backward is the same as the flat loop forward except that it is revolved to the *right* (clockwise) instead of to the left.

At the start, the rope is held in the same position. The left hand, however, can in this form of spinning be of greater assistance. The left hand can throw the loop out from the body while the right hand starts the whirl.

When the two small flat loops are mastered, left and right, some practice should be given to the left hand on the same two forms. In this way your rope spinning will result in an equal development of the many muscles brought into play by the exercise.

Twenty minutes of this work will be found to exceed the same amount of time with medium weight dumb-bells or sliding weights. The advantage lies in the fact that balancing on the balls of the feet during the spinning and the bodily adjustments required to keep the loop clear of the ground and rotating evenly, will bring into play muscles of the arms, shoulders, neck, back and legs which are probably never used as a full group except in swimming.

ROPING

There is probably no sport or exercise so valuable as rope spinning in developing close coordination of eye and muscle. The boxer, golfer, batter and many others can all profit greatly by it.

3 and 4. Flat loop—large.

We now come to the large loops in a horizontal plane. These loops are, with the 14-foot rope, about 5 feet in diameter. The spoke is about 3 feet.

If the beginner is a short person, this loop can be made somewhat smaller. A tall person with long arms can lean over and keep the loop out well clear and so use a larger one.

It is advisable to keep at the large loop until it is thoroughly mastered because from this loop evolve some of the most entertaining and fascinating tricks of the rope.

In its revolution the big loop should be just as carefully parallel to the ground as was the small loop. Its center should not oscillate back and forth; and the speed of its rotation should be varied until the roper feels a thorough master of its movement.

Here again the rhythm of the loop is important.

FIGURE 2.—FLAT LOOP—BACKWARD (RIGHT SPIN).

The flat loop backward is the same as the flat loop forward except that it is revolved to the *right* clockwise instead of to the left. (See Page 13).

THE FLAT LOOPS

One way to achieve this rhythm is for the beginner to close or half close his eyes and try to *feel* the beat, so to speak, of the *honda* as it passes a given point.

5. Big loop—over head and around body.

We now come to the first really spectacular trick of roping. In this the rope-spinner begins for the first time a trick that can develop into feats and dances such as some of the great fancy ropers like Will Rogers, Fred Stone and others have made famous.

The loop can be whirled backward or forward just as in other cases. By far the easiest way is forward or to the left. While spinning, the spoke must be allowed to turn in the hand as before to prevent kinking. In the early stages a low speed of loop is preferable.

The trick is started as given in directions above for the forward loop. Before trying the actual whirl it is well for the beginner two or three times to throw the loop about his own head, in effect lassoing himself and dropping it half way to the floor, endeavoring to have it fall spread in a regular circle. The diagram shows how this is done.

After this is practised two or three times the roper then casts the rope in such a way that the spoke is held overhead and the loop revolves from right to left equi-distantly from the body, as shown in Fig. 3—(b).

After the trick of keeping the loop going is mastered, speed should be varied, as in the case of the other loops, in order that the rhythm of the loop and the comfort of the arm in use are made the most of.

6. Big loop—around body or step-in.

In this trick the result is the same as in 5; the loop is rotated to the left and as the spoke comes around from left to right front then step in. It requires both grace and skill for perfect execution. The important thing about this method of getting the loop around the body is that the stepping-in act is the first of a series of tricks combining the motion of the body with the motion of the loop. It is the ultimate coordination of the two, body and loop, that develops the splendid exercise and diversion possible in rope spinning. (See Fig. 4.)

As in the big loop left or right the loop is held in front of the body with a large diameter, and

FIGURE 3—(a) BIG LOOP—OVER HEAD AND AROUND BODY.

Before trying the actual whirl it is well for the beginner two or three times to throw the loop about his own head, in effect lassoing himself and dropping it half way to the floor, endeavoring to have it fall spread in a regular circle. (See Page 17.)

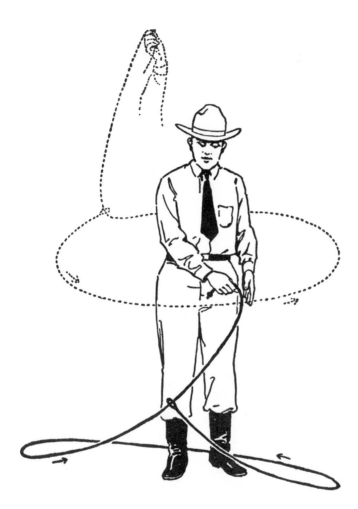

FIGURE 3—(b). BIG LOOP—OVER HEAD AND AROUND BODY.

The roper then casts the rope in such a way that the spoke is held overhead and the loop revolves from right to left equidistantly from the body, as shown in the diagram. (See Page 18.)

thrown clear for spinning. If desired, a small loop can be started and dilated by increasing its speed and lengthening the spoke. After a few seconds, usually when the loop has settled down smoothly, the roper steps in just after the spoke has passed in front of him. The reason for this is that as soon as the loop is around the body he must hoist it upward and let the spoke spin around his head as in 5. Did he step in when the spoke was at the far edge of the loop it would strike the legs or the body and so spoil the trick.

The tendency of the beginner will be to jump in with much effort. As he improves his performance he will find it easy to step lightly into the spinning loop, scarcely raising his toes off the ground. Thus the act becomes almost a dance step that is ideal for the boxer who would improve his footwork.

7. Big or small loop—passed around outside of body.

The advantage of this trick is in the exercise it gives the muscles of the trunk. It also requires a certain amount of agility and sense of rhythm in order to keep the rope spinning while it is out of sight behind the spinner.

The loop may be spun either left or right as in any of the other flat loops. It is well to begin with a small loop at first and keep its speed as slow as possible. Spin the rope with one hand for a few moments until the loop has settled down to a convenient rhythm. Then pass the loop to the opposite hand keeping the center of gravity of the loop as near the body as possible. Changes of direction are made, if possible, while the spoke is at the outer edge of the loop. In this way the tendency is to pull the loop inward while it revolves around the body as a center.

The trick may be done either to left or right and with a large loop as well as with a small one. It is much easier to have the *honda*, when on the outer edge of the loop, moving in the same direction as the center of the loop.

The trick may also be carried out with a loop well above the floor or ground and swung with the operating hand held overhead as shown in Figure 3—(b). As this form of the trick is helpful in working up some of the later tricks it is well to practise it until mastered before going on. As in many of the more intricate tricks a somewhat longer rope, say 18 feet, is desirable for this one.

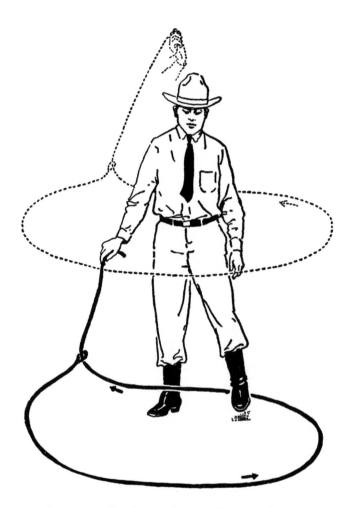

FIGURE 4.—BIG LOOP—AROUND BODY OR STEP-IN.

When the loop has settled down smoothly, the roper steps in just after the spoke has passed in front of him. (See Page 18.)

ELSIE JANIS SWINGS THE "WEDDING RING."

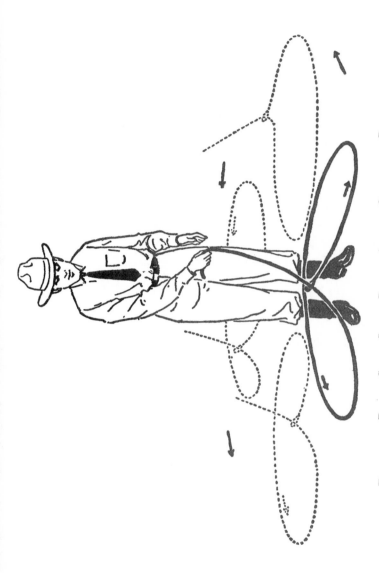

FIGURE 5.—BIG OR SMALL LOOP—PASSED AROUND OUTSIDE OF BODY.

Spin the rope with one hand for a few moments until the loop has settled down to a convenient rhythm. Then pass the loop to the opposite hand, keeping the center of gravity of the loop as near the body as possible. (See Page 30).

THE FLAT LOOPS

Another form of this trick is performed by using the loop as in 5, completely around the body, and dropping it down until close to the floor or ground. When the spoke comes to the point where it would have revolved around the head it is passed to the other hand and so on around the body as indicated in Figure 3—(b).   This is really a variation of 5.

8. Big flat loop—spoke under alternate leg.

A big loop is spun as in 5 (big loop around the body).   The loop is kept, as shown in the diagram, nearer the feet.   To prevent the spoke from wrapping around the body it is passed from hand to hand and then between the legs, first in front of the right leg, then in front of the left leg.   The other leg is lifted over the spoke.   (Fig. 6.)

This is not a skipping exercise, but it is a splendid way of developing skill in rope spinning and at the same time giving exercise to all the back and leg muscles.

9. Around the body—loop outside.

The object of this trick is to carry a flat loop clear around the body without changing hands.

Spin a flat loop forward (counter-clockwise); loop

medium size and spinning about 18 inches from the ground.

When the loop has settled down bring the right hand up over the left shoulder, pass the forearm over the head, thus carrying the loop around to the rear of the body. Continue the motion of the spinning hand so that the loop does not stop its rotation. The inner edge of the loop should be as close to the body as possible, while the loop itself is raised several feet from the ground owing to the fact that the spoke remains the same length.

As the diagram shows, the loop comes down the right side of the body resuming its original position.

This is an excellent exercise for the shoulders and trunk muscles. It may be continued as long as desired; and may be mastered readily with the left hand, spinning clockwise or to the right.

10. Up and over the head.

Spin a loop forward (counter-clockwise) a little to the right of the body and at an angle of about 45 degrees from the ground as shown.

The object of the trick is to carry this loop up and out over the left shoulder and down over the

FIGURE 6.—BIG FLAT LOOP—SPOKE UNDER ALTERNATE LEG.

To prevent the spoke from wrapping around the body it is passed from hand to hand and then between the legs, first in front of the right leg, then in front of the left leg. The other leg is lifted over the spoke. (See page 29).

FIGURE 7.—The object of the trick is to carry this loop up
over the left shoulder and down over the head so that it spins
around the body as shown by the dotted lines in the diagram.
(See page 35.)

head so that it spins around the body as shown by the dotted lines in Figure 7.

As soon as the loop has settled down carry it up to the point indicated in the diagram, at which the center of the loop is roughly several feet above the level of the head and about three feet to the left of it.

Especial care must be taken in the way the loop is lifted. If the loop is jerked upward the roper is likely to lose control. The whole motion should be one of lifting and not of jerking. The beginner is urged to try the first half of the trick a number of times before attempting to bring the loop down over the head. Move the spinning hand upward at varying rates of speed until the loop can be carried at a steady pace up to its position over the left shoulder. The trick of bringing the loop down over the body from this high point is not unlike that of carrying the loop back to the opposite side in doing the Butterfly. That is to say the spring effect of the spoke must be made use of.

In this and similar tricks the beginner will find his loop has a tendency to strike the ground or rug on which he stands and slow down. If the trick is tried on a polished floor the loop can be

allowed to touch without stopping. Incident-
ally, this business of letting the loop touch and
slip on a smooth floor will be found helpful in the
early stages of all flat-loop tricks. It steadies the
loop and gives the roper a chance to divide his
attention somewhat.

CHAPTER III

Introduction.

Vertical loops are so called because the loop revolves in a vertical plane. This form of spinning the rope is more difficult than the use of flat loops because gravity is working in a more complicated way upon the revolving loop.

In the flat loop gravity was pulling down evenly on the whole loop. Centrifugal force was carrying the loop outward. These two forces were acting evenly and consistently throughout the act of spinning.

Either a heavier *honda* should be used for making vertical loops; or weight added with a little tape just below the *honda*.

When we get into vertical spinning the loop is still dilated by centrifugal force, but the throw of the spinning hand is part of the time acting with gravity and part of the time against it. As a result we have a very much more intricate set of forces working on the loop.

The general principle of vertical spinning left or right is the same as in the flat loop. The beginner will probably find that at first it is easier to spin to the left (counter-clockwise) than to the right. He will also discover that the movement of his hand should be somewhat more pronounced in order to throw the *honda* and the rest of the loop clear.

Greater dilation of the loop by centrifugal force is just as possible in the vertical loop as in the horizontal loop. For instance, when the rope spinner reaches the point of being able to jump through the loop, he will probably start with a small loop and work it up to sufficient diameter for this trick which is described further along in the text.

1. Vertical loop—forward (left spin).

Stand as in the case of the flat loop except that the body should be bent slightly on the side on which the loop is to be spun. It is suggested that to spin the loop on the right side with the right hand will be the easiest way to start.

VERTICAL LOOPS

Hold the rope as it was held for a flat loop. Throw the rope in a circular direction using a spoke of not more than one-third the diameter of the loop. Avoid too great speed. If the loop tends to drop, let it drop down slowly and endeavor to bring it up again by increasing the speed. The spoke and all of the rope in the left hand should be allowed to turn in order to avoid kinking.

Some professional ropers prefer learning a vertical loop by spinning a flat loop and then gradually bringing the loop into a vertical plane. This is optional with the beginner. It should certainly be tried if results from the above directions prove discouraging.

Here again, as in the case with flat loops, the rope will have a tendency to kink. This nuisance can be avoided as before by spinning on alternate sides in practise and by permitting the spoke to turn in the hand.

2. Vertical loop—backward.

The vertical loop backward (to the right) is the same as vertical loop forward, except that it is thrown to the right instead of to the left.

The flat loop backward, as well as forward, should be mastered so that it can be spun with perfect ease. It is important that the roper not only get the rhythm of the loop but also learn to follow the *honda* with his eye. The reason for this is that he is approaching the time when he will alternate the right and left vertical loop in what is known as the Butterfly and Ocean Wave, two fascinating stunt forms of spinning.

Also in using the vertical loop the center of the loop should be moved up and down from about the height of the knee to about the height of the head as soon as possible, not only for the increased exercise thus given, but in order to feel at home with the loop in any position.

It is suggested also that the speed of the loop be varied. High speed gives the centrifugal force necessary to dilate and increase its size if desired. This proves useful when the roper wants to change from one trick to another. On the other hand, a slow loop is necessary in order to carry out certain forms of spinning in which perfect mastery of the loop is essential before the trick can even be attempted.

Before leaving vertical looping it should be

VERTICAL LOOPS

mastered with both left and right hands and on all sides of the body. Many have found it useful to go direct to the Butterfly, described on page 52, while working on vertical loops.

CHAPTER IV

JUMPING IN AND OUT OF A LOOP WHILE IT IS SPINNING

Introduction.

WE now come to that phase of rope spinning which is a more violent exercise and at the same time more spectacular. The beginner must not be discouraged if his progress so far has been slow. The tricks come much more quickly later on.

It has been the jumping in and out of the loop of a spinning rope that has brought this game into the public eye on the stage. Fred Stone has been one of the leading exponents of this form of rope spinning. I had the pleasure of giving him his early lessons some years ago. In his play, *The Old Town* he jumped back and forth through his spinning loop to music. The act was very popular. Of all the many stunts, performed by Fred Stone, he says this lariat dance was the one he enjoyed most.

Skipping with a spinning rope does not involve

any really new kind of rope spinning other than have been described in previous chapters. However, there are certain points in which the loops themselves differ.

For instance, a loop which is to be jumped into must be of such size that it does not foul the clothing of the roper. It must be spinning at such speed and evenness that any slight movement given it during the act of jumping will not spoil the loop. And it must be near enough the ground to require only a small jump.

It is well to practice spinning a large loop rapidly either flat or vertical and changing its speed before trying to jump in and out. The object of this preliminary work is to make it so the spinner can devote considerable attention to the actual skipping. Also it helps him adjust the speed of his loop so that he is not required to jump too rapidly.

1. Skipping with flat loop—one foot in and out.

Start a medium sized flat loop spinning in front of the body. By gradually increasing the speed of the loop dilate it until about 6 feet in diameter. A left (counter-clockwise) spin is advised in first attempts, held in the right hand.

Now let the loop slow down gradually until under full control but just clear of the ground, say 3 inches up. Bring the loop slightly to the right side of the body until the spinning hand is about opposite the right foot. Temporarily step into the loop with the right foot on the ground just as the spoke passes. This throws the weight of the body on the right foot and for a fraction of a second the roper is standing on one foot, the right one, inside the loop.

The roper now must hop partly out of the loop the same way he entered it. Before the spoke gets around to a point where it will strike the right leg his body must have been shifted to the left leg, the right foot lifted clear and the spoke allowed to pass under.

This exercise is repeated as many times as desired.

As in the other tricks, it is desirable to master this with the left hand and left foot after perfecting it on the right side. Thus muscle building through the agency of the spinning rope is kept well balanced on both sides of the body.

Principles of eliminating kinks and speed of loop as brought in flat-loop tricks, all apply.

FIGURE 8.—The spoke and hand come around in front of the body, the hand held about a foot or so to the right of the center of the body and well down. This will lower the end of the spoke near the *honda* to a point over which it can be conveniently jumped by the spinner. (See page 47.)

2. Skipping flat loop—both feet in.

This trick can be approached either by spinning the loop around the entire body as in Chapter II, section 6, or by spinning a flat loop in front of the body as in 1 above.

First we will take the easiest form, which is to spin the loop around the body.

When the loop has been spinning slowly and evenly for a few moments around the body, hand over head, the hand is dropped after the spoke has passed the left shoulder. The spoke and hand come around in front of the body, the hand held about a foot or so to the right of the center of the body and well down. This will lower the end of the spoke near the *honda* to a point over which it can be conveniently jumped by the roper. Bend quickly forward meanwhile. The jump can be made either with one foot or with both feet. Variations consist of skipping with one foot completely off the ground and then the other.

The skipping may be continued as long as desirable. An elderly person should not continue too long due to the strain on the heart.

Another way of skipping with the flat loop is nearly like that described in 1 above. The loop is first spun in front of the body and outside it, center somewhat to the right. The spinner then jumps into it just after the spoke has passed near the right leg. He then continues to hop over the revolving spoke in the manner described above.

Athletes training for a race or boxing or any other sport requiring wind will find this exercise of the utmost help. Fancy dancers depend on it to improve their grace and agility. For reducing a heavy sweater may be worn.

3. Skipping—through the vertical loop.

We now come to a point where size of rope and length are of much greater importance than before. For a 6-foot man to jump through a vertical loop his rope must be between 20 and 22 feet long and the *honda* heavy enough to open the loop to a good round circle during the spinning. As pointed out before, a good plan is to add a little tape to the rope just below the throat of the *honda*.

When the vertical loop of about 6 feet diameter has been mastered the roper is ready to begin skipping. Here again some practice must precede the actual trick.

The loop is spun first with the right hand with

the spoke about 3 feet from the *honda*. The loop should be spinning at a pretty good rate of speed.

The skip is in three moves:

(a) The right hand moves slightly away from the body as shown in the diagram carrying the loop away from the body with it. The object of this is to start the loop swinging back toward the body.

(b) The right hand is pulled in, carrying the loop back. As the spoke descends the body is turned from the loop and the shoulders dropped slightly so that there will be no chance of fouling the rope.

(c) As the loop reaches the feet the roper springs into the air and permits it to pass clear.

The roper is now facing the loop on the left hand side of his body and the loop is revolving in the new direction, counter-clockwise. This reverse in the rotation of the rope has come about just as in the Butterfly, described in Chapter V.

To jump back repeat the performance, letting the loop swing away from the body and bringing it back to give it momentum. The jump is made, as before, just after the spoke has descended and the direction of rotation reverses to clockwise on the right side.

ROPING

As shown in the diagram, the loop is kept close to the body and the hand moves in the line from one side to the other, but a few inches removed from the operator.

This trick is more difficult than either the Butterfly or Zigzag. It may, therefore, be postponed until the beginner has become more advanced in his work.

Also as skipping through the vertical loop is severe exercise if continued for some time, it should be alternated with the other tricks even after it is learned.

CHAPTER V

(Butterfly, Ocean Wave, Etc.)

Introduction.

ONE of the most discouraging things about rope spinning is the beginner's inability to keep the rope dilated and clear of the ground when trying to work out some of the tricks. So much time seems to be wasted just in untangling the rope.

Too many hours cannot be given to mastering the rhythm of the loop and the timing of the spin in such a way that the former is kept extended at all times. Before the amateur can become successful master of any of the special stunts now to be described, it is absolutely essential that he learn to *feel* the rhythm of the loop as it spins. This corresponds to the *feel* of a bat or racquet or golf club. He then can give just enough push with his spinning hand to keep the loop out without overdoing it.

ROPING

All rope spinning stunts afoot can be carried on indoors. That is one of the great attractions of the sport. When done with a small loop and at low speed rope tricks are among the most graceful feats any human being can perform. In fact, as a preface to fancy dancing they are held in high esteem by many authorities.

At the same time, done with large loops these stunts become most exhilarating exercise. It takes a strong, wiry man, for instance, to carry on the Ocean Wave for any length of time at high speed and with a large loop. The beginner's arm will soon be under the strain.

It is here in the fancy tricks for the first time that practically all muscles of the body are brought into full play at one time. The weaving in and out, the bending back and forth and the skipping, when added, combine to form a truly wonderful use of the body's many sets of muscles.

1. The Butterfly.

The Butterfly, as shown by the diagram, is simply a figure 8 with a small loop. In effect, it is the same trick as was described in the last chapter where the spinner jumped through a vertical loop.

FIGURE 9.—A loop about 3 feet in diameter is spun at the right side and in front of the body. A short length of spoke is used, say about 1 foot. The loop is spun fairly slowly, the spinning hand and wrist regulating the speed of rotation.

There are several forms of the Butterfly. The simplest is carried out as follows:

A loop about 3 feet in diameter is spun at the right side and in front of the body. A short length of spoke is used, say about 1 foot. The loop is spun fairly slowly, the spinning hand and wrist regulating the speed of rotation.

When the loop has settled down and is spinning evenly it is transferred to the left side of the body by shifting the spinning hand to the left as the spoke descends and reversing the direction of the spin from counter-clockwise to clockwise. This is an important point: *reverse with the spoke below the loop.*

The beginner would do well to spin the loop several times on each side before attempting the shift. The true Butterfly is carried out by spinning the loop just once on each side, and shifting it as the spoke comes down for the second loop. This is indicated in the diagram.

If the loop drops down and the beginner has become adept at increasing speed, he may open the loop by simply increasing its rotation.

The start is usually made by tossing the loop into a right handed spin on the left side of the body. Center of the loop should be about the height of the left shoulder. But after the spinning starts the loop is usually kept lower than the waist line. Once learned, the trick may be executed in any position.

2. The Zigzag.

The Zigzag is a form of the Butterfly. But instead of shifting the loop back and forth across the body the loop is spun in a similar way on both sides of the spinning hand. One rotation on each side is made and the shift made as the spoke descends. As in the case of the Butterfly, the Zigzag is simply a figure 8. Here again rhythm is more important than speed.

The Zigzag is easily started by giving a two-foot loop a counter-clockwise spin with the right hand. Just before the spoke reaches its lowest point a slight jerk up and to the left will give it the same rotation on the left side of the hand. Thus we have the loop spinning in two parallel planes on either side and only a few inches from the spinning hand.

3. Ocean Wave.

The Ocean Wave belongs to the class of the Butterfly and the Zigzag, but it is considerably more spectacular and certainly more difficult.

FIGURE 10.—When the loop has settled down and is spinning evenly it is transferred to the left side of the body by shifting the spinning hand to the left as the spoke descends and reversing the direction of the spin from counter-clockwise to clockwise. This is an important point: *reverse with the spoke below the loop.*

Ordinarily the Ocean Wave is thrown with a loop about 3 to 5 feet in diameter. To start with, the loop is spun right handed or clockwise in direction on the right side of the body. After a turn or two, or as soon as the loop has settled down evenly, it is carried across in front of the body much as in the case of the Butterfly or in the case of skipping through the loop. At the same time the loop is lifted higher off the ground so that the center is about opposite the left shoulder and about 3 feet distant at the extreme position on the left hand side.

The loop is now revolving in such a way as to be counter-clockwise, or left hand as viewed from the body. It is allowed to make just one full turn. During this turn the forearm is brought over the head and the loop carried far enough to the rear so as to clear the body when it is brought to the right side again by a short motion of the spinning hand. The roper thus does the vertical skipping trick, but keeps the loop outside his body.

During this whole movement the center of the loop describes a graceful curve as indicated in the diagram. It was the outline of this curve that gave the name to the stunt, the Ocean Wave.

The Ocean Wave must be carried on at a fairly

high rate of speed both in spinning and moving the loop in order to be successful. A three-foot loop is recommended for the beginner. Expert performers carry this size up to six feet.

4. Reverse Forms.

When the Butterfly, Zigzag and Ocean Wave are mastered as described above it will be found possible to attempt each in the opposite direction. That is to say, the Butterfly can be spun from the opposite direction with the rope turning counterwise from the direction and diagram above.

The beginner by all means should learn the reverse form of each trick as soon as possible and even the left-handed mastery of the trick, if possible, in order to continue the balanced exercise which has received such favorable endorsement by physical instructors.

Regarding left hand work, don't be discouraged if it seems impossible at first. The minute the left hand begins to feel the rhythm, the various tricks will begin to come easily.

5. Roll-overs. (Started from the Butterfly.)

There is almost an unlimited number of roll-overs. Ir this form of trick the spinning loop

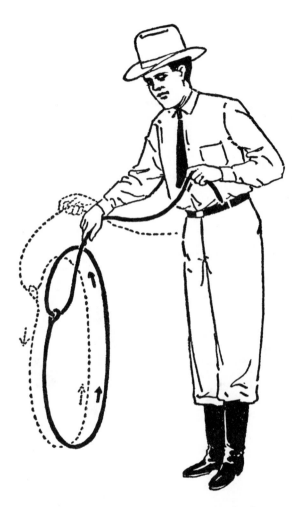

FIGURE 11.—The Zigzag is a form of the Butterfly. But instead of shifting the loop back and forth across the body the loop is spun in a similar way on both sides of the spinning hand. One rotation on each side is made and the shift made as the spoke descends. As in the case of the Butterfly, the Zigzag is simply a figure 8. Here again rhythm and speed are highly important factors.

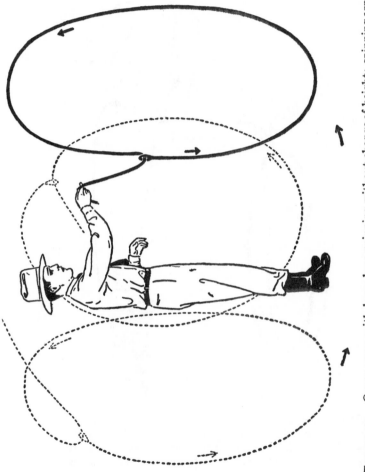

FIGURE 12.—Ocean wave with large loop spinning without change of height; spinning arm goes over head.

becomes practically a rigid article which the spinner rotates, as shown in the various diagrams, about the various parts of his body and about the spoke itself. This part of rope spinning requires a good deal of skill before it can be attempted with any hope of success.

As a matter of fact, roll-overs should not be tried until the loop has been mastered to the degree of being under perfect control at all speeds. It is more graceful and more effective to throw a roll-over with the loop rotating at low speed. Onlookers can then see every detail of the trick and the performer's full skill is obvious.

The size of the loop in roll-overs should be about 3 feet. If during the spinning the loop closes to a smaller size, the spinner should not drop the loop and open it himself but should dilate it by spinning a Butterfly or a Zigzag.

Over the forearm: The loop is spun to the left, counter-clockwise, or to the right. As shown in the diagram, the spinner throws a Butterfly, until he has the right size of loop. A Butterfly is preferable since it keeps the loop in better balance.

Then with a quick motion of the wrist and while the *honda* is on the upturn he carries the loop up and over so that its center describes a circle over the wrist and its circumference rolls like a rigid wheel gracefully up and over. The operation may be performed in either direction. The over-the-forearm can be spun either to the right or left and the principles are the same in both cases.

Over the shoulder: The start of this trick is the same as for over the forearm. The loop is brought to the right side by a series of Butterflies. It is then carried spinning to the left across the front of the body and up and over the shoulder so that it rolls gracefully and like a rigid wheel down to the opposite side. The spinning hand must carry the spoke over the head so that it does not foul. This is aided by the *honda* being on the up side of the roll as it goes over the shoulder, as is shown in the diagram. As soon as the loop drops clear it should be kept spinning by a Butterfly.

Over the spoke: This is a very difficult trick because of the interference of the body. The purpose of it is to roll the loop over the spoke, as shown in the diagram, between the two hands in such a way that it either falls in front or behind the rope. It is caught afterwards with a Butterfly as above.

64

FIGURE 13.—The loop is brought to the right side by a series of
Butterflies or Zigzags. It is then carried spinning to the left
across the front of the body and up and over the shoulder so
that it rolls gracefully and like a rigis wheel down to the opposite
side. The spinning hand must carry the spoke over the head
so that it does not foul.

FIGURE 14.—*Over the Spoke.* This is a very difficult trick because of the interference of the body. The purpose of it is to roll
the loop over the spoke, as shown in the diagram, between the
two hands in such a way that it either falls in front or behind
the rope.

The principles of starting the loop are the same as in the forearm or shoulder roll-over, except that the loop must be small enough to go through the space between the spoke and the body. The hands are held about 3 feet apart and as the loop is brought up or down between the spoke and the body, the spoke is allowed to slacken slightly in order to let the loop roll gently over.

The speed of the loop is lessened while it rolls over, not only to make it seem easier for the operator, but to permit the onlookers to get the full effect of the trick.

It will be noticed that if the loop is spun over in one direction it must be spun in the opposite direction in order to take the turn away from the spinning arm.

However, it is possible to shift the spoke in the spinning hand in such a way that the turn is taken off automatically without unwinding the loop. This part of the trick is carried out with the fingers of the spinning hand. The shift is made by the fingers before the loop is brought around so that in effect the turn is taken out before it is created. However, such requirements are not important.

Over the leg: The general principles of spinning

apply in this as in the case of the other roll-overs. The loop is kept small as in the case of rolling over the spoke.

As shown in the diagram the loop is rolled over the left leg just above the knee. In order to prevent a turn of the spoke being caught around the leg the hand must let go and catch the spoke on the opposite side as the loop falls.

The loop is spun with its center moving under the leg and then over just at the time when the *honda* is spinning upward. In this way the spoke is carried over and is coming down towards the hand when the spinning hand releases the spoke on the under side of the let. Momentum thus for a time has complete charge of the rope while the spinner is not touching it except where the loop is resting on his knee.

Over both arms: As in the case of spinning the loop over the leg a turn would be taken around the arms if the spinner did not momentarily release the loop.

The general form of the spinning and the end sought is the same as in rolling over the leg.

To prevent a turn being turned around the right arm the rope is released as in the case of the leg

FIGURE 15.—It will be noticed that if the loop is spun over in one direction it must be spun in the opposite direction in order to take the turn away from the spinning arm.

FIGURE 16.—As shown in the diagram the loop is rolled over the left leg just above the knee. In order to prevent a turn of the spoke being caught around the leg the hand must let go and catch the spoke on the opposite side as the loop falls.

roll-over. The left hand, which has been holding the unused end of the spoke, also releases its hold temporarily.

As in the case with all the other roll-overs, it is especially important that the spinner practice regaining control of the loop after the stunt has been carried out. To spin a roll-over and lose control of the rope immediately afterwards is to spoil the whole trick. For then the finished form and effect is not achieved.

Some beginners find it better to practice tricks like roll-overs a part at a time. That is, don't try the whole trick at once. Try, for instance, to throw your loop in the air towards arm, leg or shoulder, from a Butterfly. After this is done easily, then try to throw it clear over.

6. The Rolling Butterfly.

This is simply a Butterfly in which the spinning loop is thrown up and over as shown in the diagram. The alternating of the loops is the same as in the ordinary Butterfly and there is no swinging about the body as in the Ocean Wave. But the center of the loop is carried up and over in a complete circle.

ROPING

The Rolling Butterfly can be used as a beginning towards roll-overs of various sorts. The secret lies in learning to feel the exact moment when the spoke can be given a lift to throw the loop upward. This must not be a yank, but an even movement timed to blend in with the rhythm of the loop.

CHAPTER VI

HISTORY OF ROPING

THE rope spinning I am telling about in this book is a real American sport. Some say it is the greatest American sport.

A scientist looked up the origin of roping and found out it dated back to ancient Greece. Apparently soldiers of those early races used to throw ropes around their enemies. Then they would wheel their horses and drag the enemy along until he was dead.

A high brow friend of mine has dug up the following quotation from *Herodotus:*

"The Sagartians use lassoes made of thongs plaited together, and trust to these whenever they go to the wars. When they meet their enemy, straightway they discharge their lassoes, which end in a noose; then, whatever the noose encircles, be it man or be it horse, they drag towards them, and the foe, entangled in the toils, is forthwith slain."

ROPING

Will Rogers says that trick and fancy roping was brought into the United States about thirty years ago by a Mexican with Buffalo Bill's Show named Vincenti Orespo. Will ought to know. He is about the best trick and fancy roper that ever lived.

Anyway, Orespo was the first real fancy roper any of the present day living ropers saw. He couldn't do a lot of the little tricks we do now. But he was a whiz at catching horses. He always threw a small loop and put it where it belonged, around the throat latch. When he wanted a hind leg or a saddle horn he could hook that just as well.

There are a lot of names for the rope a cowboy carries on his saddle. The Mexican term is *la riata*. "*Riata*" is Spanish for rope. This was shortened to "lariat" by the Americans. We also called it a "lasso" which is really the Spanish word "*lazo*" for snare or slipknot. I guess most fellows call it just plain rope. That's what I've always called it. Anyway, they all refer to the same thing: A long line from 35 to 60 feet, for catching live stock. It can be hemp or hair.

It has always been customary to hang this coil of rope about 18 inches in diameter on some spot on the saddle below the base of the horn. It is correct to carry it on either side. It depends on whether the rider is right handed or left handed.

The rope can be made of any one of several materials. In the early days cowboys used buffalo hide braided. Sometimes rawhide was put into use. Fine hempen rope and the hair rope are probably the strongest. The latter were usually about $\frac{7}{16}$ inch in diameter. Other ropes are as thick as three-quarters of an inch. The average length of a cowboy's rope runs about 40 to 50 feet.

The loop is formed by passing the end of the rope through a *honda*. This *honda* may be a metal eyelet or one made of rawhide. Or it may simply be an eye formed by lashing back a small part of the rope upon itself. For most rope spinning a light *honda* of brass or aluminum is preferred, and the favorite material is ⅜ inch cotton braided Sampson spot cord.

I think I ought to mention something about why a rope has always been so necessary to a cowboy. You see live stock used to be turned out free range before the days of fences. Hundreds and hundreds of square miles of land were available for the cattle to roam over.   Various ranchmen knew their own cattle by brand marks.

It was necessary to round up the cattle, that is drive them into one small area, every so often in order for the stock owners to take some out and sell them; also to discover which cattle had young ones and brand these.   If there were no round-ups the herds of cattle would soon have in them full grown animals with no mark on them to show who were the owners.   That would mean trouble right off.

The average number of animals in a single bunch varied.   For horses there were usually ten to twenty-five.   For cattle the groups were even smaller and often tended to scatter.

Every spring and every fall there was held a round-up.   The Mexican word for round-up is *rodeo*.   That's why some of the contests in which cowboys now perform are called "rodeos."

In round-up season cowboys and stockmen from all the ranches bordering on a certain area would get themselves roughly organized and start out on horseback.   Their purpose was to cover such land as was grazed over by their cattle.   Sometimes enormous areas were taken into consideration, areas entirely outside those covered by the ranches themselves. Of course nowadays a man cannot work on any except his own ranch land.

To give you some idea how big this round-up job was, I'd like to say that often as many as 10,000 cattle were collected in one day's work. This is a pretty big bunch of animals.

When the great day came for the beginning of the round-up cowboys from all parts of the section of country involved, would gather together at some headquarters, maybe several headquarters. This meant that practically everybody got aboard a horse and set out. Naturally such a gathering involved a lot of renewing of friendships. That meant more celebration. If the round-up were successful that meant more celebration. The whole thing usually centered around one ranch.

As a result of all this the round-up gradually became a fine big party for all hands and usually ended in some sort of show and jubilation. The show and jubilation part developed more and more. Rivalry grew up among the cowboys of the different ranches. There got to be roping and broncho busting contests. Fancy rope spinners were developed. Horse racing came in. Even some of the cowgirls took part.

Finally, about the time I was a boy, the rodeo or round-up wasn't a true circus because in a circus you have paid entertainers. In the rodeo, which is more like an athletic meet, the entertainers were competing among themselves. Prizes were less important than success. Often success meant a better job next year.

As competition became keener and audiences more appreciative some cowboys took advantage of this chance to earn extra money. As a result many like myself have more or less gone into the thing as a business. In the right seasons we travel about the country entering "rodeos," "stampedes" and "round-ups" picking up prizes wherever we can. In between times we may hold down ranch jobs; many go back to their old work as regular cowboys. But so stiff is the competition that off seasons nowadays really mean barely enough time for a man to get into shape and training for his next set of contests.

To go back for a moment to the round-ups will show how the rope is used in a practical way.

When stock animals are herded together in a

mass it becomes necessary to single out those due for market and the young calves to be branded. Thus two kinds of singling out work have been specially developed: steer roping and calf roping.

The steer or calf must be separated from the herd by what is called "cutting out." This means that the rider approaches the herd and finds the animal he wants to get hold of. By approaching this animal with his horse, he gradually edges it toward the outside. His pony must be trained to understand what its rider is after. The minute the steer or calf realizes that he is being moved away from his family and friends he does his darnedest to go back. He gets sort of hysterical. He begins to run and dodge and even fight. Here is where the "cut out" pony has got to be right on the job.

By the time the steer or calf is well clear of the herd the main fun begins. Everything is now done at top speed. Both animals are at full gallop and darting to and fro for all they are worth. The pony's eyes follow every movement of the quarry. His eagerness shows how much fun he gets out of the job.

With lightning-like rapidity shifts of direction

are made.   The cowboy in the meantime seizes his rope from his saddle and throws out the loop to be ready.   He doesn't whirl it yet.   He mustn't catch his animal too soon or the branders might become involved in the herd.   He has got to chase him well clear.

I must say that the average rider would not even be able to stick on during this period, so unexpected and rapid are the movements of a well trained horse.   And don't forget the lariat must be kept clear.

The rope is jerked out gradually until its loop is about 8 feet in diameter.   A skilful roper sometimes uses even a smaller loop.   Then he starts swinging.   The loop spreads out, that is dilates, until it is somewhere near circular.

All this has to be done while the pony is still twisting and turning.   If anybody thinks it is easy let him try it.   It is hard enough to keep a rope spinning on the ground.   Of course the cowboy has to carry his throwing arm well back so that when he lets go he can give the rope a real throw.

He watches his chance.   Then with a quick swing of his right hand he sends the loop circling out near the head or under the legs of the calf or steer.

The cowboy and pony must now separate. By a jerk either with the rope or by yanking on the steer's tail the captured animal is up ended and flung on its side. It is the pony's job to stand with firm legs and not give the steer a chance to get on his feet again. The rider dismounts and takes care of his captive, finally turning him over to the branding party.

In this work it was not necessary to use trick rope spinning. So long as a man could throw a well opened loop and place it accurately that was about all that was needed.

While there is no record of it, it is likely that modern trick and fancy rope spinning developed when cowboys were back at the ranch house straightening out their ropes. Possibly in untangling them and softening them up a certain amount of spinning was naturally done. At any rate, as time went on more and more tricks for handling a spinning loop were devised. Some of these tricks were impossible for a mounted rider. Only a very few had anything directly to do with the capture of cattle.

Nowadays all rodeos and round-ups have their fancy roping contests. Some of the best men have even gone on the stage. I think Will Rogers has been able to hold his audiences as much by the magic way he handles his rope as by his wit.

Be sure to understand that trick roping is absolutely different from spinning. Trick roping is the act of catching an animal by throwing some sort of loop. A "catch" must always be made in this. Rope spinning is complete in itself. That is to say, rotating a loop of rope at various speeds, making it take different shapes and positions is both a sport and exercise that is only indirectly related to the popular idea of the use of the westerner's lasso.

Trick roping stunts on horseback are most entertaining and are very difficult not only because they require skill with rope but also good control of the horse. I have seen a long lariat thrown to catch four to eight horses. I have seen a running horse caught by all four feet. Some cowboys throw blindfolded. And so on.

The rope spinning that I describe in this book does not include any such tricks as the above. A person can spin a rope in his house as well as outdoors. That is the great advantage of it as compared with tennis or golf. I have a friend who takes his rope when he goes off traveling.   He tells me he spins it in the morning and at night at the beginning and end of each day.   This, he declares, gives him fine exercise and keeps his weight down to normal.   Also, he claims, it is a fine thing for his digestion because it uses all his trunk muscles.

CHAPTER VII

MY LIFE

I WAS born in Knoxville, Illinois, in 1892. I left Knoxville at the age of about three and went to Mulhall, Oklahoma. This was my first real taste of the great open West.

I remember my father taking me out walking in Mulhall. We used to meet men riding into town all fitted out with chaps and ropes and big hats.

My father would point them out as the cowboys off surrounding ranches. They were fine sun-tanned fellows always talking and laughing. The more I looked at them the more they appealed to me. I thought if I could grow up to be a cowboy it would be the most wonderful thing in the world. Business or mechanics had no appeal to me.

One day when I was about eight years old I saw a cowboy ride in who was named Will Rogers. Since that day he has become known to most everybody in the United States, if not in the whole world.

I think what really started me off in the rope spinning business was an older lad named Clyde

Miller.   He had learned to spin a rope by associating with some of the cowboys.   He could throw it around his body and do some fancy tricks that opened the eyes of us younger boys.

On day Clyde showed me how to put a rope together, splice in an eye and fix the end so that it would not unravel.

There was another boy named Sam Garrett, who also got interested in rope spinning.   Sam was a sort of partner of mine.   In fact he stuck along with me in the show business until recent years. Sam's grandfather was in the cold storage business and used to deliver stuff with an old blind horse. Every time we got a chance we used to "borrow" the horse and go off on a roping expedition.   The blind horse acted as target.

I guess we made ourselves a terrible nuisance to the neighbors as we used to rope everything in sight—cows, roosters, dogs and even cats when we could catch them.   The tricks Clyde Miller taught us in spinning a rope were a great help on these roping parties.   We found if we could open the loop and get it under control before we threw it we had a much better chance of catching our animal.

Of course I found out in later years that this was

the principle of all roping.   The many cowboys I
have known, certainly the best among them, were
usually masters of rope spinning and often used it
in their work.   As a rule a man develops several
tricks of his own that he can do better than anyone else.

I figured out as soon as I got through school I
would go into the show business.   It seemed to me
that if I could spin a rope in a snappy way other
people would be interested in watching me.   In
fact the way Clyde Miller used to draw a crowd
sometimes was proof right before my eyes how
true this was.   One of the secrets of a successful
trick is to suggest that anyone in the audience
could do it.

My first job came in the spring of 1905.   Old
Major Gordon W. Lillie, known as "Pawnee Bill,"
came to Guthrie, Oklahoma, with his show.

Clyde Miller and I had been looking at some of
the advertisements.   Suddenly he said to me,
"Come on, Chet, let's join that show."

"Do you mean it?" said I.

"Absolutely.   What say?"

That conversation was about all we needed to
set us off, so we shipped on down to Guthrie with

a couple of dollars in our pockets and got the Major to take us on. He wasn't very enthusiastic about our rope spinning, but he said he'd take a chance.

I was pretty worried because I hadn't told my folks about it. However, I thought if I could make good and collect some money they would be so pleased they wouldn't mind.

But luck was against me. I came down with a fever and after being pretty low for about three weeks I had to go home.

I remember my father didn't say very much when I got back. But there wasn't any doubt about the way he felt. Certainly I was ashamed of myself for the whole thing. I felt as if I had absolutely failed.

During the same summer, after I had recovered, I had another chance. Colonel Zack Mulhall, the well-known showman, came along one day and offered to take me up to the big show; the show was known as the "Buffalo Chase" at 101 Ranch near Bliss, Oklahoma. Bliss is now known as Marland. That show was one of the first modern rodeos ever held in the United States. It was a whiz.

I had never seen such a crowd in my life before. Trains were coming in from every direction bringing mobs of people. That was before the days when everybody owned an automobile or could go into the movies. So the show naturally attracted a lot of people. It was held in an enormous field over 50 acres in extent. The real purpose was to depict western life of about a generation before. There were the prairie schooners and broncho busting and rope spinning of all sorts. I took part in the last named. I didn't make much money. But I got a good line on what other ropers could do. Some were so good that I was a little disheartened. Would I ever equal them? I set my teeth and determined to practise until my arm dropped off. That was my only chance.

Sam Garrett and I from then on worked together as partners. One of the things we did during the ensuing months was to go around to the anti-horse thief association meetings and do our stuff. It strikes me curious, now that I think of it, that Will Rogers used to collect a crowd during the war when the Liberty Loan drives were on. His rope spinning helped collect money against a common enemy just as the spinning that Sam and I used to do also helped collect money against an enemy of society.

MY LIFE

In 1907 I went out on my first real tour with a thrilling show. I was only fifteen years old. Zack Mulhall was the boss of the gang. The name of the act was *Lucille Mulhall's Congress of Rough Riders.* This act made a great hit every performance. We had a movable corral which was suspended up in the drops. Before our act ended at each performance the corral was lowered down on the stage.

The act opened with Martin Van Bergen coming out on the back of a horse and singing *Annie Laurie* in a fine baritone voice. I guess this song got Lucille after a while for he finally married her. Then the rest of us fellows did a number of rope spinning stunts. When the corral came down from overhead at the end of the act a leading man or snubber brought in a bucking broncho. There were always a lot of feminine screams in the audience when this happened. We had two of these animals—one was named Buzzard-X and the other Johnny-on-the-Spot. Meanwhile the audience was being introduced to Charlie Mulhall and Jack Joyce who then went in and mounted the broncho—not both at the same time, but whosever turn it was for the performance. We gave two shows a day so this team had to alternate. The only trouble was that sometimes the bronchos got sort of bored and wouldn't act up. That took a lot of pep out of the show.

All of us in this act lived in the same town. This made the party a friendly one. And we were very successful. So after cruising around through the East we broke up early in the spring in Chicago and all went home pretty well heeled.

The next year I joined up with the Pawnee Bill Show in Pawnee, Oklahoma. This was a sort of Wild West show that was getting ready to leave for the East. The Buffalo Bill outfit had already made a great hit. Pretty soon things looked right to the old man so we boarded our train, horses and all, and headed for Boston. I tell you those New Englanders certainly opened their eyes when we landed in that Massachusetts town. And the season was a triumph from end to end.

From Boston I went West again and joined one of the pleasantest shows of my career on Lucky Baldwin's ranch outside of Los Angeles. That reminds me: One day Fred Stone came down from the city where he was playing. He said: "I want you to teach me some new stuff, Byers, and I want to brush up on some of the things I know."

Well, you know how Fred Stone is—one of the most persuasive fellows in the world. He pried me loose from the Lucky Baldwin outfit and got me to go with him for about eight weeks.

I guess there are few men in the world today who are as persistent and industrious in anything they start as Fred Stone. He certainly is a living lesson in determination. If he began to learn a trick I don't think he would hesitate to practice it a million times over and over again if that were necessary to master it. And the nice thing about him, too, is that he is so human. You would think all this determination in his character would make him grim. That's not so. He is a regular fellow if there ever was one.

Next I went down to New Orleans and tied up with the Miller Brothers' 101 Ranch Show backed by the ranch of that name. We made a circuit down through Mexico and played in old Mexico City for a while. This was one of the most interesting trips I ever made because I always felt our audiences knew what we were about. It was quite different from playing in certain sections where many of the onlookers didn't known the difference between a pump handle and a saddle horn. I made a lot of friends in this outfit and was with the show off and on until 1914.

Soon after this I went to South America and landed in Rio de Janeiro on my way to Buenos Aires where we opened in the forepart of November and played at the Palmo Chico eight weeks. From there we went to Rosario. During a stay of three weeks there was what they called a locust storm. It came up in the afternoon about 3:30 just like a big storm off in the distance; within 35 or 40 minutes the locusts appeared over us in a terrible swarm. When everything had cleared away they had eaten all the grass, rosebuds, and other vegetation just like any crop pest. After that I couldn't feel easy in that country.

From there we went to Montevideo, Uruguay, where we played six weeks; then to Santos, Brazil, on our way home. Then we came back to Rio de Janeiro where we sailed for New York.

In between seasons I traveled around through the West picking up some odd money and amusing myself here and there. For instance, I remember the Los Angeles rodeo in the spring of 1911 was a

pretty fine performance.   This was one of the first
real rodeos I ever attended.   Then I took a turn
up North and went into the Pendleton Round-up at
Pendleton, Oregon.   This is now held annually
and is probably the greatest rodeo in the world.

In the summer of 1914 the 101-Ranch Show went
to England.   There was a place outside of London
called The White City in those days just like the
Wembley Show held in 1924.   I think the English
people understood and liked us almost better than
the average Americans because they understood
and liked horsemanship.   Of course, being English-
men, they didn't seem to get as excited about it
all as an American would.   But they certainly
appreciated what we could do with our animals
and our ropes.

Early in August we suddenly found interest in
our party going down.   The first thing we knew
war had broken out.   The rest of the fellows and
myself talked things over and in one jump hopped
across to Pendleton, Oregon, pretty close to 6,000
miles west and south.

I had banged around in the world a good deal
by this time and began to feel a little homesick.
So after the Pendleton Round-up I went down to

Oklahoma City where my family had moved and spent some time with my father and mother. The old folks were always pretty sorry that I didn't stay at home and hold down a town job where they could see me every day. I don't blame them. But that's the way with life.

In August, 1916, I came East with a large crowd of western ranchmen, cowboys and others for what was known as a "Stampede," to be held at Sheepshead Bay. I'd like to say here that when you come right down to it, Stampedes, Rodeos, Round-ups and Frontier Days all mean about the same thing. These terms refer to shows and set forth the horsemanship and roping ability that has been developed in our great West during the past hundred years. Such shows were in the last generation held at the ranches only. They were held when the season for round-up came and the cowboys all got together to celebrate. But shrewd business men saw the profitable showmanship in such parties. As a result rodeos and round-ups are now held from one end of the United States to the other.

Harry Harkness and a group of rich men who liked horses brought us all on to Sheepshead Bay.

Guy Weadick was the promoter for this show. A lot of famous men took a keen interest in what went on. I remember seeing Theodore Roosevelt come into the ring one day and look over the horses and men. Will Rogers was there with bells on; and a lot of other notables. I guess Will would like to have been out in the arena himself instead of just looking on.

Up until early in 1919 I spent a good deal of my time with the 101-Ranch Show which also included the Buffalo Bill Show. You know a promoter got hold of the Buffalo Bill name and was able to use it with full rights from the estate. Jess Willard made some money in his prize fighting and finally bought out the 101-Ranch Show.

By this time I began to feel pretty sure of myself in both my show and my roping. I had been at the game now for 13 years. Most of the time I had been either traveling or performing as a member of some show. I concluded to go out for myself.

It was a nice feeling of freedom after I had made this decision. I could now work when and how I pleased, once I had picked my show. My own big job was to please the public. I had learned by experience that if I could really please the public I always pleased the man I was under contract to.

In doing this individual work I was acting the part of a contestant rather than just an exhibitor. That is to say, I pitted my skill against the skill of the rest of the fellows who had entered. Sometimes the contest was one of cowboys' trick and fancy roping. Other times it was a question of seeing how quick one could rope and tie a steer or a calf. Naturally I entered all the contests I could in order to make my work as profitable as possible.

My first rodeo under the new condition was at Medicine Hat, Alberta, in July, 1918. It wasn't a big show and I wasn't called on to stretch myself. But I must say I enjoyed the new layout in feeling I was in for myself.

I won't go into the many details of what a rodeo or round-up is like at this point. But I will say that the growing popularity of these shows has kept me on the jump in the last eight years. I have entered in contests at Pendleton, Fort Worth, Denver, Tulsa, Cheyenne, Dewey, Okla., Oklahoma City, Philadelphia, Chicago, New York, Birmingham, Belle Fourche, South Dakota, Calgary, Alberta, Cedar Rapids, Iowa, Salt Lake City,

Bozeman, Mont., El Paso, Tex., Tucson, Ariz., and so on. This shows how the idea of cowboy contests has grown in recent years.

Most of these shows are held in the summer time when the weather is good. This has to be the case, also, because the men who take part are not paid performers. They finance their own transportation and that of their horses. They come to enter the athletic contests just as a group of golf stars go to the big tournaments. The remuneration in the way of prizes is the bait which draws us. Naturally the fact that contestants are not paid performers elimates the possibility that the contests are "sold out" before they start. No one knows ahead of time who is going to win. And there is always a good hot struggle between entrants. This tends to keep the sport clean and exciting.

Most of us lie off in the winter months getting ready for the early spring shows. I say lie off, but I don't mean take it easy. Because there is a whole lot of training and preparation that must be gone through with in the way of roping calves and other exercise before we are in shape to start a new season. Then there are the horses to be considered. If these aren't up in top notch shape they will fail just as men would fail.   They must be carefully fed and kept and regularly exercised.   They must be also kept in close touch with any tricks which their owners are going to perform in order that they may not be made nervous by unexpected happenings.

What am I going to do in the future?   Pretty much the same thing, I guess.   But I hope to do it in a bigger way.   I have this hope because I believe in the work I am doing.   The enthusiasm that has been shown in recent years for the rodeo and other forms of cowboy shows convinces me that the American public is recognizing what a fine clean sport all this is.   I believe it is only a question of a few years before rope spinning and other forms of roping will enter the arena of amateur sport shoulder to shoulder with baseball, golf, tennis and swimming.   Certainly there is no more stimulating and all round healthful pastime than that which I am describing in this book and which can be carried to extraordinary limits when taken up in connection with horsemanship.

LIST OF

MEN TRICK AND FANCY ROPERS

Fred Burns
Vincenti Orespo
Will Rogers
Frank Chambers
Be Ho Gray
John Judd
Sam Garrett
Tom Kirnan
Fred Stone
Sy Compton
Tex McLoud
Jack Joyce
Guy Weadick

Bob Calen
Lenord Stroud
D. V. Tantlingler
Candy Hammer
Johnny Rufus
Hank Durnell
Harry Greer
Jack Webb
Cuba Crutchfield
Buff Jones
Chuck Hass
Geo. "Fig" Newton
Gordon Jones

LADY FANCY ROPERS

Lucille Mulhall
Hazel Moran
Elsie Janis
Mrs. D. V. Tantlingler

Mrs. "Florence Ladue"
Guy Weadick
Helen Walker
Tilley Bowman

Pearl Gist

BOY FANCY ROPERS

McFarland Boys
Blatherwick

GIRL FANCY ROPERS

Norman Sisters
Blatherwick

A CATALOG OF SELECTED
DOVER BOOKS
IN ALL FIELDS OF INTEREST

A CATALOG OF SELECTED DOVER
BOOKS IN ALL FIELDS OF INTEREST

CONCERNING THE SPIRITUAL IN ART, Wassily Kandinsky. Pioneering work by father of abstract art. Thoughts on color theory, nature of art. Analysis of earlier masters. 12 illustrations. 80pp. of text. 5⅜ x 8½. 23411-8 Pa. $4.95

ANIMALS: 1,419 Copyright-Free Illustrations of Mammals, Birds, Fish, Insects, etc., Jim Harter (ed.). Clear wood engravings present, in extremely lifelike poses, over 1,000 species of animals. One of the most extensive pictorial sourcebooks of its kind. Captions. Index. 284pp. 9 x 12. 23766-4 Pa. $14.95

CELTIC ART: The Methods of Construction, George Bain. Simple geometric techniques for making Celtic interlacements, spirals, Kells-type initials, animals, humans, etc. Over 500 illustrations. 160pp. 9 x 12. (Available in U.S. only.) 22923-8 Pa. $9.95

AN ATLAS OF ANATOMY FOR ARTISTS, Fritz Schider. Most thorough reference work on art anatomy in the world. Hundreds of illustrations, including selections from works by Vesalius, Leonardo, Goya, Ingres, Michelangelo, others. 593 illustrations. 192pp. 7⅛ x 10¼. 20241-0 Pa. $9.95

CELTIC HAND STROKE-BY-STROKE (Irish Half-Uncial from "The Book of Kells"): An Arthur Baker Calligraphy Manual, Arthur Baker. Complete guide to creating each letter of the alphabet in distinctive Celtic manner. Covers hand position, strokes, pens, inks, paper, more. Illustrated. 48pp. 8¼ x 11. 24336-2 Pa. $3.95

EASY ORIGAMI, John Montroll. Charming collection of 32 projects (hat, cup, pelican, piano, swan, many more) specially designed for the novice origami hobbyist. Clearly illustrated easy-to-follow instructions insure that even beginning papercrafters will achieve successful results. 48pp. 8¼ x 11. 27298-2 Pa. $3.50

THE COMPLETE BOOK OF BIRDHOUSE CONSTRUCTION FOR WOODWORKERS, Scott D. Campbell. Detailed instructions, illustrations, tables. Also data on bird habitat and instinct patterns. Bibliography. 3 tables. 63 illustrations in 15 figures. 48pp. 5¼ x 8½. 24407-5 Pa. $2.50

BLOOMINGDALE'S ILLUSTRATED 1886 CATALOG: Fashions, Dry Goods and Housewares, Bloomingdale Brothers. Famed merchants' extremely rare catalog depicting about 1,700 products: clothing, housewares, firearms, dry goods, jewelry, more. Invaluable for dating, identifying vintage items. Also, copyright-free graphics for artists, designers. Co-published with Henry Ford Museum & Greenfield Village. 160pp. 8¼ x 11. 25780-0 Pa. $10.95

HISTORIC COSTUME IN PICTURES, Braun & Schneider. Over 1,450 costumed figures in clearly detailed engravings–from dawn of civilization to end of 19th century. Captions. Many folk costumes. 256pp. 8⅜ x 11¾. 23150-X Pa. $12.95

STICKLEY CRAFTSMAN FURNITURE CATALOGS, Gustav Stickley and L. & J. G. Stickley. Beautiful, functional furniture in two authentic catalogs from 1910. 594 illustrations, including 277 photos, show settles, rockers, armchairs, reclining chairs, bookcases, desks, tables. 183pp. 6½ x 9¼. 23838-5 Pa. $11.95

AMERICAN LOCOMOTIVES IN HISTORIC PHOTOGRAPHS: 1858 to 1949, Ron Ziel (ed.). A rare collection of 126 meticulously detailed official photographs, called "builder portraits," of American locomotives that majestically chronicle the rise of steam locomotive power in America. Introduction. Detailed captions. xi+ 129pp. 9 x 12. 27393-8 Pa. $13.95

AMERICA'S LIGHTHOUSES: An Illustrated History, Francis Ross Holland, Jr. Delightfully written, profusely illustrated fact-filled survey of over 200 American lighthouses since 1716. History, anecdotes, technological advances, more. 240pp. 8 x 10¾. 25576-X Pa. $12.95

TOWARDS A NEW ARCHITECTURE, Le Corbusier. Pioneering manifesto by founder of "International School." Technical and aesthetic theories, views of industry, economics, relation of form to function, "mass-production split" and much more. Profusely illustrated. 320pp. 6⅛ x 9¼. (Available in U.S. only.) 25023-7 Pa. $10.95

HOW THE OTHER HALF LIVES, Jacob Riis. Famous journalistic record, exposing poverty and degradation of New York slums around 1900, by major social reformer. 100 striking and influential photographs. 233pp. 10 x 7⅞. 22012-5 Pa. $11.95

FRUIT KEY AND TWIG KEY TO TREES AND SHRUBS, William M. Harlow. One of the handiest and most widely used identification aids. Fruit key covers 120 deciduous and evergreen species; twig key 160 deciduous species. Easily used. Over 300 photographs. 126pp. 5⅜ x 8½. 20511-8 Pa. $3.95

COMMON BIRD SONGS, Dr. Donald J. Borror. Songs of 60 most common U.S. birds: robins, sparrows, cardinals, bluejays, finches, more—arranged in order of increasing complexity. Up to 9 variations of songs of each species.
Cassette and manual 99911-4 $8.95

ORCHIDS AS HOUSE PLANTS, Rebecca Tyson Northen. Grow cattleyas and many other kinds of orchids—in a window, in a case, or under artificial light. 63 illustrations. 148pp. 5⅜ x 8½. 23261-1 Pa. $7.95

MONSTER MAZES, Dave Phillips. Masterful mazes at four levels of difficulty. Avoid deadly perils and evil creatures to find magical treasures. Solutions for all 32 exciting illustrated puzzles. 48pp. 8¼ x 11. 26005-4 Pa. $2.95

MOZART'S DON GIOVANNI (DOVER OPERA LIBRETTO SERIES), Wolfgang Amadeus Mozart. Introduced and translated by Ellen H. Bleiler. Standard Italian libretto, with complete English translation. Convenient and thoroughly portable—an ideal companion for reading along with a recording or the performance itself. Introduction. List of characters. Plot summary. 121pp. 5¼ x 8½. 24944-1 Pa. $3.95

TECHNICAL MANUAL AND DICTIONARY OF CLASSICAL BALLET, Gail Grant. Defines, explains, comments on steps, movements, poses and concepts. 15-page pictorial section. Basic book for student, viewer. 127pp. 5⅜ x 8½. 21843-0 Pa. $4.95

THE CLARINET AND CLARINET PLAYING, David Pino. Lively, comprehensive work features suggestions about technique, musicianship, and musical interpretation, as well as guidelines for teaching, making your own reeds, and preparing for public performance. Includes an intriguing look at clarinet history. "A godsend," *The Clarinet,* Journal of the International Clarinet Society. Appendixes. 7 illus. 320pp. 5⅜ x 8½. 40270-3 Pa. $9.95

HOLLYWOOD GLAMOR PORTRAITS, John Kobal (ed.). 145 photos from 1926-49. Harlow, Gable, Bogart, Bacall; 94 stars in all. Full background on photographers, technical aspects. 160pp. 8⅜ x 11¼. 23352-9 Pa. $12.95

THE ANNOTATED CASEY AT THE BAT: A Collection of Ballads about the Mighty Casey/Third, Revised Edition, Martin Gardner (ed.). Amusing sequels and parodies of one of America's best-loved poems: Casey's Revenge, Why Casey Whiffed, Casey's Sister at the Bat, others. 256pp. 5⅜ x 8½. 28598-7 Pa. $8.95

THE RAVEN AND OTHER FAVORITE POEMS, Edgar Allan Poe. Over 40 of the author's most memorable poems: "The Bells," "Ulalume," "Israfel," "To Helen," "The Conqueror Worm," "Eldorado," "Annabel Lee," many more. Alphabetic lists of titles and first lines. 64pp. 5³⁄₁₆ x 8¼. 26685-0 Pa. $1.00

PERSONAL MEMOIRS OF U. S. GRANT, Ulysses Simpson Grant. Intelligent, deeply moving firsthand account of Civil War campaigns, considered by many the finest military memoirs ever written. Includes letters, historic photographs, maps and more. 528pp. 6⅛ x 9¼. 28587-1 Pa. $12.95

ANCIENT EGYPTIAN MATERIALS AND INDUSTRIES, A. Lucas and J. Harris. Fascinating, comprehensive, thoroughly documented text describes this ancient civilization's vast resources and the processes that incorporated them in daily life, including the use of animal products, building materials, cosmetics, perfumes and incense, fibers, glazed ware, glass and its manufacture, materials used in the mummification process, and much more. 544pp. 6⅛ x 9¼. (Available in U.S. only.) 40446-3 Pa. $16.95

RUSSIAN STORIES/PYCCKNE PACCKA3bl: A Dual-Language Book, edited by Gleb Struve. Twelve tales by such masters as Chekhov, Tolstoy, Dostoevsky, Pushkin, others. Excellent word-for-word English translations on facing pages, plus teaching and study aids, Russian/English vocabulary, biographical/critical introductions, more. 416pp. 5⅜ x 8½. 26244-8 Pa. $9.95

PHILADELPHIA THEN AND NOW: 60 Sites Photographed in the Past and Present, Kenneth Finkel and Susan Oyama. Rare photographs of City Hall, Logan Square, Independence Hall, Betsy Ross House, other landmarks juxtaposed with contemporary views. Captures changing face of historic city. Introduction. Captions. 128pp. 8¼ x 11. 25790-8 Pa. $9.95

AIA ARCHITECTURAL GUIDE TO NASSAU AND SUFFOLK COUNTIES, LONG ISLAND, The American Institute of Architects, Long Island Chapter, and the Society for the Preservation of Long Island Antiquities. Comprehensive, well-researched and generously illustrated volume brings to life over three centuries of Long Island's great architectural heritage. More than 240 photographs with authoritative, extensively detailed captions. 176pp. 8¼ x 11. 26946-9 Pa. $14.95

NORTH AMERICAN INDIAN LIFE: Customs and Traditions of 23 Tribes, Elsie Clews Parsons (ed.). 27 fictionalized essays by noted anthropologists examine religion, customs, government, additional facets of life among the Winnebago, Crow, Zuni, Eskimo, other tribes. 480pp. 6⅛ x 9¼. 27377-6 Pa. $10.95

CATALOG OF DOVER BOOKS

FRANK LLOYD WRIGHT'S DANA HOUSE, Donald Hoffmann. Pictorial essay of residential masterpiece with over 160 interior and exterior photos, plans, elevations, sketches and studies. 128pp. 9¹/₄ x 10¾. 29120-0 Pa. $14.95

THE MALE AND FEMALE FIGURE IN MOTION: 60 Classic Photographic Sequences, Eadweard Muybridge. 60 true-action photographs of men and women walking, running, climbing, bending, turning, etc., reproduced from rare 19th-century masterpiece. vi + 121pp. 9 x 12. 24745-7 Pa. $12.95

1001 QUESTIONS ANSWERED ABOUT THE SEASHORE, N. J. Berrill and Jacquelyn Berrill. Queries answered about dolphins, sea snails, sponges, starfish, fishes, shore birds, many others. Covers appearance, breeding, growth, feeding, much more. 305pp. 5¼ x 8¼. 23366-9 Pa. $9.95

ATTRACTING BIRDS TO YOUR YARD, William J. Weber. Easy-to-follow guide offers advice on how to attract the greatest diversity of birds: birdhouses, feeders, water and waterers, much more. 96pp. 5³/₁₆ x 8¼. 28927-3 Pa. $2.50

MEDICINAL AND OTHER USES OF NORTH AMERICAN PLANTS: A Historical Survey with Special Reference to the Eastern Indian Tribes, Charlotte Erichsen-Brown. Chronological historical citations document 500 years of usage of plants, trees, shrubs native to eastern Canada, northeastern U.S. Also complete identifying information. 343 illustrations. 544pp. 6½ x 9¼. 25951-X Pa. $12.95

STORYBOOK MAZES, Dave Phillips. 23 stories and mazes on two-page spreads: Wizard of Oz, Treasure Island, Robin Hood, etc. Solutions. 64pp. 8¼ x 11. 23628-5 Pa. $2.95

AMERICAN NEGRO SONGS: 230 Folk Songs and Spirituals, Religious and Secular, John W. Work. This authoritative study traces the African influences of songs sung and played by black Americans at work, in church, and as entertainment. The author discusses the lyric significance of such songs as "Swing Low, Sweet Chariot," "John Henry," and others and offers the words and music for 230 songs. Bibliography. Index of Song Titles. 272pp. 6¹/₂ x 9¹/₄. 40271-1 Pa. $9.95

MOVIE-STAR PORTRAITS OF THE FORTIES, John Kobal (ed.). 163 glamor, studio photos of 106 stars of the 1940s: Rita Hayworth, Ava Gardner, Marlon Brando, Clark Gable, many more. 176pp. 8⅜ x 11¼. 23546-7 Pa. $14.95

BENCHLEY LOST AND FOUND, Robert Benchley. Finest humor from early 30s, about pet peeves, child psychologists, post office and others. Mostly unavailable elsewhere. 73 illustrations by Peter Arno and others. 183pp. 5⅜ x 8½. 22410-4 Pa. $6.95

YEKL and THE IMPORTED BRIDEGROOM AND OTHER STORIES OF YIDDISH NEW YORK, Abraham Cahan. Film Hester Street based on *Yekl* (1896). Novel, other stories among first about Jewish immigrants on N.Y.'s East Side. 240pp. 5⅜ x 8½. 22427-9 Pa. $7.95

SELECTED POEMS, Walt Whitman. Generous sampling from *Leaves of Grass*. Twenty-four poems include "I Hear America Singing," "Song of the Open Road," "I Sing the Body Electric," "When Lilacs Last in the Dooryard Bloom'd," "O Captain! My Captain!"–all reprinted from an authoritative edition. Lists of titles and first lines. 128pp. 5³/₁₆ x 8¼. 26878-0 Pa. $1.00

THE BEST TALES OF HOFFMANN, E. T. A. Hoffmann. 10 of Hoffmann's most important stories: "Nutcracker and the King of Mice," "The Golden Flowerpot," etc. 458pp. 5⅜ x 8½. 21793-0 Pa. $9.95

FROM FETISH TO GOD IN ANCIENT EGYPT, E. A. Wallis Budge. Rich detailed survey of Egyptian conception of "God" and gods, magic, cult of animals, Osiris, more. Also, superb English translations of hymns and legends. 240 illustrations. 545pp. 5⅜ x 8½. 25803-3 Pa. $13.95

FRENCH STORIES/CONTES FRANÇAIS: A Dual-Language Book, Wallace Fowlie. Ten stories by French masters, Voltaire to Camus: "Micromegas" by Voltaire; "The Atheist's Mass" by Balzac; "Minuet" by de Maupassant; "The Guest" by Camus, six more. Excellent English translations on facing pages. Also French-English vocabulary list, exercises, more. 352pp. 5⅜ x 8½. 26443-2 Pa. $9.95

CHICAGO AT THE TURN OF THE CENTURY IN PHOTOGRAPHS: 122 Historic Views from the Collections of the Chicago Historical Society, Larry A. Viskochil. Rare large-format prints offer detailed views of City Hall, State Street, the Loop, Hull House, Union Station, many other landmarks, circa 1904-1913. Introduction. Captions. Maps. 144pp. 9⅜ x 12¼. 24656-6 Pa. $12.95

OLD BROOKLYN IN EARLY PHOTOGRAPHS, 1865-1929, William Lee Younger. Luna Park, Gravesend race track, construction of Grand Army Plaza, moving of Hotel Brighton, etc. 157 previously unpublished photographs. 165pp. 8⅞ x 11¾. 23587-4 Pa. $13.95

THE MYTHS OF THE NORTH AMERICAN INDIANS, Lewis Spence. Rich anthology of the myths and legends of the Algonquins, Iroquois, Pawnees and Sioux, prefaced by an extensive historical and ethnological commentary. 36 illustrations. 480pp. 5⅜ x 8½. 25967-6 Pa. $10.95

AN ENCYCLOPEDIA OF BATTLES: Accounts of Over 1,560 Battles from 1479 B.C. to the Present, David Eggenberger. Essential details of every major battle in recorded history from the first battle of Megiddo in 1479 B.C. to Grenada in 1984. List of Battle Maps. New Appendix covering the years 1967-1984. Index. 99 illustrations. 544pp. 6½ x 9¼. 24913-1 Pa. $16.95

SAILING ALONE AROUND THE WORLD, Captain Joshua Slocum. First man to sail around the world, alone, in small boat. One of great feats of seamanship told in delightful manner. 67 illustrations. 294pp. 5⅜ x 8½. 20326-3 Pa. $6.95

ANARCHISM AND OTHER ESSAYS, Emma Goldman. Powerful, penetrating, prophetic essays on direct action, role of minorities, prison reform, puritan hypocrisy, violence, etc. 271pp. 5⅜ x 8½. 22484-8 Pa. $8.95

MYTHS OF THE HINDUS AND BUDDHISTS, Ananda K. Coomaraswamy and Sister Nivedita. Great stories of the epics; deeds of Krishna, Shiva, taken from puranas, Vedas, folk tales; etc. 32 illustrations. 400pp. 5⅜ x 8½. 21759-0 Pa. $12.95

THE TRAUMA OF BIRTH, Otto Rank. Rank's controversial thesis that anxiety neurosis is caused by profound psychological trauma which occurs at birth. 256pp. 5⅜ x 8½. 27974-X Pa. $7.95

A THEOLOGICO-POLITICAL TREATISE, Benedict Spinoza. Also contains unfinished Political Treatise. Great classic on religious liberty, theory of government on common consent. R. Elwes translation. Total of 421pp. 5⅜ x 8½. 20249-6 Pa. $10.95

MY BONDAGE AND MY FREEDOM, Frederick Douglass. Born a slave, Douglass became outspoken force in antislavery movement. The best of Douglass' autobiographies. Graphic description of slave life. 464pp. 5⅜ x 8½. 22457-0 Pa. $8.95

FOLLOWING THE EQUATOR: A Journey Around the World, Mark Twain. Fascinating humorous account of 1897 voyage to Hawaii, Australia, India, New Zealand, etc. Ironic, bemused reports on peoples, customs, climate, flora and fauna, politics, much more. 197 illustrations. 720pp. 5⅜ x 8½. 26113-1 Pa. $15.95

THE PEOPLE CALLED SHAKERS, Edward D. Andrews. Definitive study of Shakers: origins, beliefs, practices, dances, social organization, furniture and crafts, etc. 33 illustrations. 351pp. 5⅜ x 8½. 21081-2 Pa. $12.95

THE MYTHS OF GREECE AND ROME, H. A. Guerber. A classic of mythology, generously illustrated, long prized for its simple, graphic, accurate retelling of the principal myths of Greece and Rome, and for its commentary on their origins and significance. With 64 illustrations by Michelangelo, Raphael, Titian, Rubens, Canova, Bernini and others. 480pp. 5⅜ x 8½. 27584-1 Pa. $10.95

PSYCHOLOGY OF MUSIC, Carl E. Seashore. Classic work discusses music as a medium from psychological viewpoint. Clear treatment of physical acoustics, auditory apparatus, sound perception, development of musical skills, nature of musical feeling, host of other topics. 88 figures. 408pp. 5⅜ x 8½. 21851-1 Pa. $11.95

THE PHILOSOPHY OF HISTORY, Georg W. Hegel. Great classic of Western thought develops concept that history is not chance but rational process, the evolution of freedom. 457pp. 5⅜ x 8½. 20112-0 Pa. $9.95

THE BOOK OF TEA, Kakuzo Okakura. Minor classic of the Orient: entertaining, charming explanation, interpretation of traditional Japanese culture in terms of tea ceremony. 94pp. 5⅜ x 8½. 20070-1 Pa. $3.95

LIFE IN ANCIENT EGYPT, Adolf Erman. Fullest, most thorough, detailed older account with much not in more recent books, domestic life, religion, magic, medicine, commerce, much more. Many illustrations reproduce tomb paintings, carvings, hieroglyphs, etc. 597pp. 5⅜ x 8½. 22632-8 Pa. $12.95

SUNDIALS, Their Theory and Construction, Albert Waugh. Far and away the best, most thorough coverage of ideas, mathematics concerned, types, construction, adjusting anywhere. Simple, nontechnical treatment allows even children to build several of these dials. Over 100 illustrations. 230pp. 5⅜ x 8½. 22947-5 Pa. $8.95

THEORETICAL HYDRODYNAMICS, L. M. Milne-Thomson. Classic exposition of the mathematical theory of fluid motion, applicable to both hydrodynamics and aerodynamics. Over 600 exercises. 768pp. 6⅛ x 9¼. 68970-0 Pa. $20.95

SONGS OF EXPERIENCE: Facsimile Reproduction with 26 Plates in Full Color, William Blake. 26 full-color plates from a rare 1826 edition. Includes "TheTyger," "London," "Holy Thursday," and other poems. Printed text of poems. 48pp. 5¼ x 7. 24636-1 Pa. $4.95

OLD-TIME VIGNETTES IN FULL COLOR, Carol Belanger Grafton (ed.). Over 390 charming, often sentimental illustrations, selected from archives of Victorian graphics—pretty women posing, children playing, food, flowers, kittens and puppies, smiling cherubs, birds and butterflies, much more. All copyright-free. 48pp. 9¼ x 12¼. 27269-9 Pa. $7.95

PERSPECTIVE FOR ARTISTS, Rex Vicat Cole. Depth, perspective of sky and sea, shadows, much more, not usually covered. 391 diagrams, 81 reproductions of drawings and paintings. 279pp. 5⅜ x 8½. 22487-2 Pa. $9.95

DRAWING THE LIVING FIGURE, Joseph Sheppard. Innovative approach to artistic anatomy focuses on specifics of surface anatomy, rather than muscles and bones. Over 170 drawings of live models in front, back and side views, and in widely varying poses. Accompanying diagrams. 177 illustrations. Introduction. Index. 144pp. 8⅜ x11¼. 26723-7 Pa. $9.95

GOTHIC AND OLD ENGLISH ALPHABETS: 100 Complete Fonts, Dan X. Solo. Add power, elegance to posters, signs, other graphics with 100 stunning copyright-free alphabets: Blackstone, Dolbey, Germania, 97 more–including many lower-case, numerals, punctuation marks. 104pp. 8⅛ x 11. 24695-7 Pa. $9.95

HOW TO DO BEADWORK, Mary White. Fundamental book on craft from simple projects to five-bead chains and woven works. 106 illustrations. 142pp. 5⅜ x 8. 20697-1 Pa. $5.95

THE BOOK OF WOOD CARVING, Charles Marshall Sayers. Finest book for beginners discusses fundamentals and offers 34 designs. "Absolutely first rate . . . well thought out and well executed."–E. J. Tangerman. 118pp. 7¾ x 10⅝. 23654-4 Pa. $7.95

ILLUSTRATED CATALOG OF CIVIL WAR MILITARY GOODS: Union Army Weapons, Insignia, Uniform Accessories, and Other Equipment, Schuyler, Hartley, and Graham. Rare, profusely illustrated 1846 catalog includes Union Army uniform and dress regulations, arms and ammunition, coats, insignia, flags, swords, rifles, etc. 226 illustrations. 160pp. 9 x 12. 24939-5 Pa. $12.95

WOMEN'S FASHIONS OF THE EARLY 1900s: An Unabridged Republication of "New York Fashions, 1909," National Cloak & Suit Co. Rare catalog of mail-order fashions documents women's and children's clothing styles shortly after the turn of the century. Captions offer full descriptions, prices. Invaluable resource for fashion, costume historians. Approximately 725 illustrations. 128pp. 8⅜ x 11¼. 27276-1 Pa. $12.95

THE 1912 AND 1915 GUSTAV STICKLEY FURNITURE CATALOGS, Gustav Stickley. With over 200 detailed illustrations and descriptions, these two catalogs are essential reading and reference materials and identification guides for Stickley furniture. Captions cite materials, dimensions and prices. 112pp. 6½ x 9¼. 26676-1 Pa. $9.95

EARLY AMERICAN LOCOMOTIVES, John H. White, Jr. Finest locomotive engravings from early 19th century: historical (1804–74), main-line (after 1870), special, foreign, etc. 147 plates. 142pp. 11⅜ x 8¼. 22772-3 Pa. $12.95

THE TALL SHIPS OF TODAY IN PHOTOGRAPHS, Frank O. Braynard. Lavishly illustrated tribute to nearly 100 majestic contemporary sailing vessels: Amerigo Vespucci, Clearwater, Constitution, Eagle, Mayflower, Sea Cloud, Victory, many more. Authoritative captions provide statistics, background on each ship. 190 black-and-white photographs and illustrations. Introduction. 128pp. 8⅞ x 11¾. 27163-3 Pa. $14.95

LITTLE BOOK OF EARLY AMERICAN CRAFTS AND TRADES, Peter Stockham (ed.). 1807 children's book explains crafts and trades: baker, hatter, cooper, potter, and many others. 23 copperplate illustrations. 140pp. $4^{5}/_{8}$ x 6.
23336-7 Pa. $4.95

VICTORIAN FASHIONS AND COSTUMES FROM HARPER'S BAZAR, 1867–1898, Stella Blum (ed.). Day costumes, evening wear, sports clothes, shoes, hats, other accessories in over 1,000 detailed engravings. 320pp. 9⅜ x 12¼.
22990-4 Pa. $16.95

GUSTAV STICKLEY, THE CRAFTSMAN, Mary Ann Smith. Superb study surveys broad scope of Stickley's achievement, especially in architecture. Design philosophy, rise and fall of the Craftsman empire, descriptions and floor plans for many Craftsman houses, more. 86 black-and-white halftones. 31 line illustrations. Introduction 208pp. 6½ x 9¼.
27210-9 Pa. $9.95

THE LONG ISLAND RAIL ROAD IN EARLY PHOTOGRAPHS, Ron Ziel. Over 220 rare photos, informative text document origin (1844) and development of rail service on Long Island. Vintage views of early trains, locomotives, stations, passengers, crews, much more. Captions. 8⅞ x 11¾.
26301-0 Pa. $14.95

VOYAGE OF THE LIBERDADE, Joshua Slocum. Great 19th-century mariner's thrilling, first-hand account of the wreck of his ship off South America, the 35-foot boat he built from the wreckage, and its remarkable voyage home. 128pp. 5⅜ x 8½.
40022-0 Pa. $5.95

TEN BOOKS ON ARCHITECTURE, Vitruvius. The most important book ever written on architecture. Early Roman aesthetics, technology, classical orders, site selection, all other aspects. Morgan translation. 331pp. 5⅜ x 8½.   20645-9 Pa. $9.95

THE HUMAN FIGURE IN MOTION, Eadweard Muybridge. More than 4,500 stopped-action photos, in action series, showing undraped men, women, children jumping, lying down, throwing, sitting, wrestling, carrying, etc. 390pp. 7⅞ x 10⅝.
20204-6 Clothbd. $29.95

TREES OF THE EASTERN AND CENTRAL UNITED STATES AND CANADA, William M. Harlow. Best one-volume guide to 140 trees. Full descriptions, woodlore, range, etc. Over 600 illustrations. Handy size. 288pp. 4½ x 6⅜.
20395-6 Pa. $6.95

SONGS OF WESTERN BIRDS, Dr. Donald J. Borror. Complete song and call repertoire of 60 western species, including flycatchers, juncoes, cactus wrens, many more—includes fully illustrated booklet.   Cassette and manual 99913-0 $8.95

GROWING AND USING HERBS AND SPICES, Milo Miloradovich. Versatile handbook provides all the information needed for cultivation and use of all the herbs and spices available in North America. 4 illustrations. Index. Glossary. 236pp. 5⅜ x 8½.
25058-X Pa. $7.95

BIG BOOK OF MAZES AND LABYRINTHS, Walter Shepherd. 50 mazes and labyrinths in all—classical, solid, ripple, and more—in one great volume. Perfect inexpensive puzzler for clever youngsters. Full solutions. 112pp. 8⅛ x 11.
22951-3 Pa. $5.95

PIANO TUNING, J. Cree Fischer. Clearest, best book for beginner, amateur. Simple repairs, raising dropped notes, tuning by easy method of flattened fifths. No previous skills needed. 4 illustrations. 201pp. 5⅜ x 8½.   23267-0 Pa. $6.95

HINTS TO SINGERS, Lillian Nordica. Selecting the right teacher, developing confidence, overcoming stage fright, and many other important skills receive thoughtful discussion in this indispensible guide, written by a world-famous diva of four decades' experience. 96pp. 5³/₈ x 8¹/₂.   40094-8 Pa. $4.95

THE COMPLETE NONSENSE OF EDWARD LEAR, Edward Lear. All nonsense limericks, zany alphabets, Owl and Pussycat, songs, nonsense botany, etc., illustrated by Lear. Total of 320pp. 5⅜ x 8½. (Available in U.S. only.)   20167-8 Pa. $7.95

VICTORIAN PARLOUR POETRY: An Annotated Anthology, Michael R. Turner. 117 gems by Longfellow, Tennyson, Browning, many lesser-known poets. "The Village Blacksmith," "Curfew Must Not Ring Tonight," "Only a Baby Small," dozens more, often difficult to find elsewhere. Index of poets, titles, first lines. xxiii + 325pp. 5⅜ x 8¼.   27044-0 Pa. $12.95

DUBLINERS, James Joyce. Fifteen stories offer vivid, tightly focused observations of the lives of Dublin's poorer classes. At least one, "The Dead," is considered a masterpiece. Reprinted complete and unabridged from standard edition. 160pp. 5³/₁₆ x 8¼.   26870-5 Pa. $1.50

GREAT WEIRD TALES: 14 Stories by Lovecraft, Blackwood, Machen and Others, S. T. Joshi (ed.). 14 spellbinding tales, including "The Sin Eater," by Fiona McLeod, "The Eye Above the Mantel," by Frank Belknap Long, as well as renowned works by R. H. Barlow, Lord Dunsany, Arthur Machen, W. C. Morrow and eight other masters of the genre. 256pp. 5⅜ x 8½. (Available in U.S. only.)   40436-6 Pa. $8.95

THE BOOK OF THE SACRED MAGIC OF ABRAMELIN THE MAGE, translated by S. MacGregor Mathers. Medieval manuscript of ceremonial magic. Basic document in Aleister Crowley, Golden Dawn groups. 268pp. 5⅜ x 8½.   23211-5 Pa. $9.95

NEW RUSSIAN-ENGLISH AND ENGLISH-RUSSIAN DICTIONARY, M. A. O'Brien. This is a remarkably handy Russian dictionary, containing a surprising amount of information, including over 70,000 entries. 366pp. 4½ x 6⅛.   20208-9 Pa. $10.95

HISTORIC HOMES OF THE AMERICAN PRESIDENTS, Second, Revised Edition, Irvin Haas. A traveler's guide to American Presidential homes, most open to the public, depicting and describing homes occupied by every American President from George Washington to George Bush. With visiting hours, admission charges, travel routes. 175 photographs. Index. 160pp. 8¼ x 11.   26751-2 Pa. $13.95

NEW YORK IN THE FORTIES, Andreas Feininger. 162 brilliant photographs by the well-known photographer, formerly with *Life* magazine. Commuters, shoppers, Times Square at night, much else from city at its peak. Captions by John von Hartz. 181pp. 9¼ x 10¾.   23585-8 Pa. $13.95

INDIAN SIGN LANGUAGE, William Tomkins. Over 525 signs developed by Sioux and other tribes. Written instructions and diagrams. Also 290 pictographs. 111pp. 6⅛ x 9¼.   22029-X Pa. $3.95

ANATOMY: A Complete Guide for Artists, Joseph Sheppard. A master of figure drawing shows artists how to render human anatomy convincingly. Over 460 illustrations. 224pp. 8⅜ x 11¼. 27279-6 Pa. $11.95

MEDIEVAL CALLIGRAPHY: Its History and Technique, Marc Drogin. Spirited history, comprehensive instruction manual covers 13 styles (ca. 4th century through 15th). Excellent photographs; directions for duplicating medieval techniques with modern tools. 224pp. 8⅜ x 11¼. 26142-5 Pa. $12.95

DRIED FLOWERS: How to Prepare Them, Sarah Whitlock and Martha Rankin. Complete instructions on how to use silica gel, meal and borax, perlite aggregate, sand and borax, glycerine and water to create attractive permanent flower arrangements. 12 illustrations. 32pp. 5⅜ x 8½. 21802-3 Pa. $1.00

EASY-TO-MAKE BIRD FEEDERS FOR WOODWORKERS, Scott D. Campbell. Detailed, simple-to-use guide for designing, constructing, caring for and using feeders. Text, illustrations for 12 classic and contemporary designs. 96pp. 5⅜ x 8½. 25847-5 Pa. $3.95

SCOTTISH WONDER TALES FROM MYTH AND LEGEND, Donald A. Mackenzie. 16 lively tales tell of giants rumbling down mountainsides, of a magic wand that turns stone pillars into warriors, of gods and goddesses, evil hags, powerful forces and more. 240pp. 5⅜ x 8½. 29677-6 Pa. $6.95

THE HISTORY OF UNDERCLOTHES, C. Willett Cunnington and Phyllis Cunnington. Fascinating, well-documented survey covering six centuries of English undergarments, enhanced with over 100 illustrations: 12th-century laced-up bodice, footed long drawers (1795), 19th-century bustles, l9th-century corsets for men, Victorian "bust improvers," much more. 272pp. 5⅜ x 8¼. 27124-2 Pa. $9.95

ARTS AND CRAFTS FURNITURE: The Complete Brooks Catalog of 1912, Brooks Manufacturing Co. Photos and detailed descriptions of more than 150 now very collectible furniture designs from the Arts and Crafts movement depict davenports, settees, buffets, desks, tables, chairs, bedsteads, dressers and more, all built of solid, quarter-sawed oak. Invaluable for students and enthusiasts of antiques, Americana and the decorative arts. 80pp. 6½ x 9¼. 27471-3 Pa. $8.95

WILBUR AND ORVILLE: A Biography of the Wright Brothers, Fred Howard. Definitive, crisply written study tells the full story of the brothers' lives and work. A vividly written biography, unparalleled in scope and color, that also captures the spirit of an extraordinary era. 560pp. 6⅛ x 9¼. 40297-5 Pa. $17.95

THE ARTS OF THE SAILOR: Knotting, Splicing and Ropework, Hervey Garrett Smith. Indispensable shipboard reference covers tools, basic knots and useful hitches; handsewing and canvas work, more. Over 100 illustrations. Delightful reading for sea lovers. 256pp. 5⅜ x 8½. 26440-8 Pa. $8.95

FRANK LLOYD WRIGHT'S FALLINGWATER: The House and Its History, Second, Revised Edition, Donald Hoffmann. A total revision–both in text and illustrations–of the standard document on Fallingwater, the boldest, most personal architectural statement of Wright's mature years, updated with valuable new material from the recently opened Frank Lloyd Wright Archives. "Fascinating"–*The New York Times*. 116 illustrations. 128pp. 9¼ x 10¾. 27430-6 Pa. $12.95

PHOTOGRAPHIC SKETCHBOOK OF THE CIVIL WAR, Alexander Gardner. 100 photos taken on field during the Civil War. Famous shots of Manassas Harper's Ferry, Lincoln, Richmond, slave pens, etc. 244pp. 10⅝ x 8¼.   22731-6 Pa. $10.95

FIVE ACRES AND INDEPENDENCE, Maurice G. Kains. Great back-to-the-land classic explains basics of self-sufficient farming. The one book to get. 95 illustrations. 397pp. 5⅜ x 8½.   20974-1 Pa. $7.95

SONGS OF EASTERN BIRDS, Dr. Donald J. Borror. Songs and calls of 60 species most common to eastern U.S.: warblers, woodpeckers, flycatchers, thrushes, larks, many more in high-quality recording.   Cassette and manual 99912-2 $9.95

A MODERN HERBAL, Margaret Grieve. Much the fullest, most exact, most useful compilation of herbal material. Gigantic alphabetical encyclopedia, from aconite to zedoary, gives botanical information, medical properties, folklore, economic uses, much else. Indispensable to serious reader. 161 illustrations. 888pp. 6½ x 9¼. 2-vol. set. (Available in U.S. only.)   Vol. I: 22798-7 Pa. $10.95
Vol. II: 22799-5 Pa. $10.95

HIDDEN TREASURE MAZE BOOK, Dave Phillips. Solve 34 challenging mazes accompanied by heroic tales of adventure. Evil dragons, people-eating plants, blood-thirsty giants, many more dangerous adversaries lurk at every twist and turn. 34 mazes, stories, solutions. 48pp. 8¼ x 11.   24566-7 Pa. $2.95

LETTERS OF W. A. MOZART, Wolfgang A. Mozart. Remarkable letters show bawdy wit, humor, imagination, musical insights, contemporary musical world; includes some letters from Leopold Mozart. 276pp. 5⅜ x 8½.   22859-2 Pa. $9.95

BASIC PRINCIPLES OF CLASSICAL BALLET, Agrippina Vaganova. Great Russian theoretician, teacher explains methods for teaching classical ballet. 118 illustrations. 175pp. 5⅜ x 8½.   22036-2 Pa. $6.95

THE JUMPING FROG, Mark Twain. Revenge edition. The original story of The Celebrated Jumping Frog of Calaveras County, a hapless French translation, and Twain's hilarious "retranslation" from the French. 12 illustrations. 66pp. 5⅜ x 8½.
22686-7 Pa. $4.95

BEST REMEMBERED POEMS, Martin Gardner (ed.). The 126 poems in this superb collection of 19th- and 20th-century British and American verse range from Shelley's "To a Skylark" to the impassioned "Renascence" of Edna St. Vincent Millay and to Edward Lear's whimsical "The Owl and the Pussycat." 224pp. 5⅜ x 8½.
27165-X Pa. $5.95

COMPLETE SONNETS, William Shakespeare. Over 150 exquisite poems deal with love, friendship, the tyranny of time, beauty's evanescence, death and other themes in language of remarkable power, precision and beauty. Glossary of archaic terms. 80pp. 5³⁄₁₆ x 8¼.   26686-9 Pa. $1.00

THE BATTLES THAT CHANGED HISTORY, Fletcher Pratt. Eminent historian profiles 16 crucial conflicts, ancient to modern, that changed the course of civilization. 352pp. 5⅜ x 8½.   41129-X Pa. $9.95

THE WIT AND HUMOR OF OSCAR WILDE, Alvin Redman (ed.). More than 1,000 ripostes, paradoxes, wisecracks: Work is the curse of the drinking classes; I can resist everything except temptation; etc. 258pp. 5⅜ x 8½. 20602-5 Pa. $6.95

SHAKESPEARE LEXICON AND QUOTATION DICTIONARY, Alexander Schmidt. Full definitions, locations, shades of meaning in every word in plays and poems. More than 50,000 exact quotations. 1,485pp. 6½ x 9¼. 2-vol. set.
Vol. 1: 22726-X Pa. $17.95
Vol. 2: 22727-8 Pa. $17.95

SELECTED POEMS, Emily Dickinson. Over 100 best-known, best-loved poems by one of America's foremost poets, reprinted from authoritative early editions. No comparable edition at this price. Index of first lines. 64pp. $5\frac{3}{16}$ x 8¼. 26466-1 Pa. $1.00

THE INSIDIOUS DR. FU-MANCHU, Sax Rohmer. The first of the popular mystery series introduces a pair of English detectives to their archnemesis, the diabolical Dr. Fu-Manchu. Flavorful atmosphere, fast-paced action, and colorful characters enliven this classic of the genre. 208pp. $5\frac{3}{16}$ x 8¼. 29898-1 Pa. $2.00

THE MALLEUS MALEFICARUM OF KRAMER AND SPRENGER, translated by Montague Summers. Full text of most important witchhunter's "bible," used by both Catholics and Protestants. 278pp. 6⅝ x 10. 22802-9 Pa. $12.95

SPANISH STORIES/CUENTOS ESPAÑOLES: A Dual-Language Book, Angel Flores (ed.). Unique format offers 13 great stories in Spanish by Cervantes, Borges, others. Faithful English translations on facing pages. 352pp. 5⅜ x 8½. 25399-6 Pa. $8.95

GARDEN CITY, LONG ISLAND, IN EARLY PHOTOGRAPHS, 1869–1919, Mildred H. Smith. Handsome treasury of 118 vintage pictures, accompanied by carefully researched captions, document the Garden City Hotel fire (1899), the Vanderbilt Cup Race (1908), the first airmail flight departing from the Nassau Boulevard Aerodrome (1911), and much more. 96pp. 8⅞ x 11¾. 40669-5 Pa. $12.95

OLD QUEENS, N.Y., IN EARLY PHOTOGRAPHS, Vincent F. Seyfried and William Asadorian. Over 160 rare photographs of Maspeth, Jamaica, Jackson Heights, and other areas. Vintage views of DeWitt Clinton mansion, 1939 World's Fair and more. Captions. 192pp. 8⅞ x 11. 26358-4 Pa. $14.95

CAPTURED BY THE INDIANS: 15 Firsthand Accounts, 1750-1870, Frederick Drimmer. Astounding true historical accounts of grisly torture, bloody conflicts, relentless pursuits, miraculous escapes and more, by people who lived to tell the tale. 384pp. 5⅜ x 8½. 24901-8 Pa. $9.95

THE WORLD'S GREAT SPEECHES (Fourth Enlarged Edition), Lewis Copeland, Lawrence W. Lamm, and Stephen J. McKenna. Nearly 300 speeches provide public speakers with a wealth of updated quotes and inspiration–from Pericles' funeral oration and William Jennings Bryan's "Cross of Gold Speech" to Malcolm X's powerful words on the Black Revolution and Earl of Spenser's tribute to his sister, Diana, Princess of Wales. 944pp. 5⅜ x 8⅜. 40903-1 Pa. $15.95

THE BOOK OF THE SWORD, Sir Richard F. Burton. Great Victorian scholar/adventurer's eloquent, erudite history of the "queen of weapons"–from prehistory to early Roman Empire. Evolution and development of early swords, variations (sabre, broadsword, cutlass, scimitar, etc.), much more. 336pp. 6⅛ x 9¼. 25434-8 Pa. $9.95

AUTOBIOGRAPHY: The Story of My Experiments with Truth, Mohandas K. Gandhi. Boyhood, legal studies, purification, the growth of the Satyagraha (nonviolent protest) movement. Critical, inspiring work of the man responsible for the freedom of India. 480pp. 5⅜ x 8½. (Available in U.S. only.) 24593-4 Pa. $9.95

CELTIC MYTHS AND LEGENDS, T. W. Rolleston. Masterful retelling of Irish and Welsh stories and tales. Cuchulain, King Arthur, Deirdre, the Grail, many more. First paperback edition. 58 full-page illustrations. 512pp. 5⅜ x 8½. 26507-2 Pa. $9.95

THE PRINCIPLES OF PSYCHOLOGY, William James. Famous long course complete, unabridged. Stream of thought, time perception, memory, experimental methods; great work decades ahead of its time. 94 figures. 1,391pp. 5⅜ x 8½. 2-vol. set.
Vol. I: 20381-6 Pa. $14.95
Vol. II: 20382-4 Pa. $14.95

THE WORLD AS WILL AND REPRESENTATION, Arthur Schopenhauer. Definitive English translation of Schopenhauer's life work, correcting more than 1,000 errors, omissions in earlier translations. Translated by E. F. J. Payne. Total of 1,269pp. 5⅜ x 8½. 2-vol. set.
Vol. 1: 21761-2 Pa. $12.95
Vol. 2: 21762-0 Pa. $12.95

MAGIC AND MYSTERY IN TIBET, Madame Alexandra David-Neel. Experiences among lamas, magicians, sages, sorcerers, Bonpa wizards. A true psychic discovery. 32 illustrations. 321pp. 5⅜ x 8½. (Available in U.S. only.) 22682-4 Pa. $9.95

THE EGYPTIAN BOOK OF THE DEAD, E. A. Wallis Budge. Complete reproduction of Ani's papyrus, finest ever found. Full hieroglyphic text, interlinear transliteration, word-for-word translation, smooth translation. 533pp. 6½ x 9¼.
21866-X Pa. $12.95

MATHEMATICS FOR THE NONMATHEMATICIAN, Morris Kline. Detailed, college-level treatment of mathematics in cultural and historical context, with numerous exercises. Recommended Reading Lists. Tables. Numerous figures. 641pp. 5⅜ x 8½.
24823-2 Pa. $11.95

PROBABILISTIC METHODS IN THE THEORY OF STRUCTURES, Isaac Elishakoff. Well-written introduction covers the elements of the theory of probability from two or more random variables, the reliability of such multivariable structures, the theory of random function, Monte Carlo methods of treating problems incapable of exact solution, and more. Examples. 502pp. $5^{3}/_{8}$ x $8^{1}/_{2}$. 40691-1 Pa. $16.95

THE RIME OF THE ANCIENT MARINER, Gustave Doré, S. T. Coleridge. Doré's finest work; 34 plates capture moods, subtleties of poem. Flawless full-size reproductions printed on facing pages with authoritative text of poem. "Beautiful. Simply beautiful."–*Publisher's Weekly.* 77pp. 9¼ x 12. 22305-1 Pa. $7.95

NORTH AMERICAN INDIAN DESIGNS FOR ARTISTS AND CRAFTSPEOPLE, Eva Wilson. Over 360 authentic copyright-free designs adapted from Navajo blankets, Hopi pottery, Sioux buffalo hides, more. Geometrics, symbolic figures, plant and animal motifs, etc. 128pp. 8⅜ x 11. (Not for sale in the United Kingdom.) 25341-4 Pa. $9.95

SCULPTURE: Principles and Practice, Louis Slobodkin. Step-by-step approach to clay, plaster, metals, stone; classical and modern. 253 drawings, photos. 255pp. 8⅛ x 11.
22960-2 Pa. $11.95

THE INFLUENCE OF SEA POWER UPON HISTORY, 1660–1783, A. T. Mahan. Influential classic of naval history and tactics still used as text in war colleges. First paperback edition. 4 maps. 24 battle plans. 640pp. 5⅜ x 8½.   25509-3 Pa. $14.95

THE STORY OF THE TITANIC AS TOLD BY ITS SURVIVORS, Jack Winocour (ed.). What it was really like. Panic, despair, shocking inefficiency, and a little heroism. More thrilling than any fictional account. 26 illustrations. 320pp. 5⅜ x 8½.
20610-6 Pa. $8.95

FAIRY AND FOLK TALES OF THE IRISH PEASANTRY, William Butler Yeats (ed.). Treasury of 64 tales from the twilight world of Celtic myth and legend: "The Soul Cages," "The Kildare Pooka," "King O'Toole and his Goose," many more. Introduction and Notes by W. B. Yeats. 352pp. 5⅜ x 8½.   26941-8 Pa. $8.95

BUDDHIST MAHAYANA TEXTS, E. B. Cowell and others (eds.). Superb, accurate translations of basic documents in Mahayana Buddhism, highly important in history of religions. The Buddha-karita of Asvaghosha, Larger Sukhavativyuha, more. 448pp. 5⅜ x 8½.   25552-2 Pa. $12.95

ONE TWO THREE . . . INFINITY: Facts and Speculations of Science, George Gamow. Great physicist's fascinating, readable overview of contemporary science: number theory, relativity, fourth dimension, entropy, genes, atomic structure, much more. 128 illustrations. Index. 352pp. 5⅜ x 8½.   25664-2 Pa. $9.95

EXPERIMENTATION AND MEASUREMENT, W. J. Youden. Introductory manual explains laws of measurement in simple terms and offers tips for achieving accuracy and minimizing errors. Mathematics of measurement, use of instruments, experimenting with machines. 1994 edition. Foreword. Preface. Introduction. Epilogue. Selected Readings. Glossary. Index. Tables and figures. 128pp. $5^{3}/_{8}$ x $8^{1}/_{2}$.
40451-X Pa. $6.95

DALÍ ON MODERN ART: The Cuckolds of Antiquated Modern Art, Salvador Dalí. Influential painter skewers modern art and its practitioners. Outrageous evaluations of Picasso, Cézanne, Turner, more. 15 renderings of paintings discussed. 44 calligraphic decorations by Dalí. 96pp. 5⅜ x 8½. (Available in U.S. only.)   29220-7 Pa. $5.95

ANTIQUE PLAYING CARDS: A Pictorial History, Henry René D'Allemagne. Over 900 elaborate, decorative images from rare playing cards (14th–20th centuries): Bacchus, death, dancing dogs, hunting scenes, royal coats of arms, players cheating, much more. 96pp. 9¼ x 12¼.   29265-7 Pa. $12.95

MAKING FURNITURE MASTERPIECES: 30 Projects with Measured Drawings, Franklin H. Gottshall. Step-by-step instructions, illustrations for constructing handsome, useful pieces, among them a Sheraton desk, Chippendale chair, Spanish desk, Queen Anne table and a William and Mary dressing mirror. 224pp. 8⅛ x 11¼.
29338-6 Pa. $13.95

THE FOSSIL BOOK: A Record of Prehistoric Life, Patricia V. Rich et al. Profusely illustrated definitive guide covers everything from single-celled organisms and dinosaurs to birds and mammals and the interplay between climate and man. Over 1,500 illustrations. 760pp. 7½ x 10⅛.   29371-8 Pa. $29.95

Prices subject to change without notice.

Available at your book dealer or write for free catalog to Dept. GI, Dover Publications, Inc., 31 East 2nd St., Mineola, N.Y. 11501. Dover publishes more than 500 books each year on science, elementary and advanced mathematics, biology, music, art, literary history, social sciences and other areas.